INTRODUCTION TO MODERN FINANCE:

15 Principles

By

Stéphane Reverre

ISBN: 978-2-9565764-1-9

Edited and Formatted by Self-Publishing Services LLC.

www.SelfPublishingServices.com

To my loved ones for their patience and support.

Table of Contents

Introduction

This book is born out of a long-held belief: modern finance, particularly the capital markets, is unintelligible for most people. The financial crisis that erupted in 2008 with the bankruptcy of Lehman Brothers has triggered an unprecedented economic crisis and turned the spotlight on the traders of large international banks, how much they earn and, of course, the degree to which they were responsible for what happened.

And yet the sophistication of products and the advent of quantitative finance have transformed the world and enabled considerable progress. During the 19th century, only the national (and later multinational) capital markets could have financed the colossal investments required to develop the railways, trade and transportation. Would the industrial revolution have been possible without a mature, reasonably efficient capitalism capable of innovation? A century later, the internet would never have become what it is today without sophisticated and fluid capital (and therefore risk) circulation mechanisms which have enabled visionary entrepreneurs to create digital empires largely comparable to John D. Rockefeller's Standard Oil 100 years earlier.

Warren Buffett, renowned for his proverbial wisdom and sky-high returns to shareholders, has described derivatives as "weapons of mass destruction"[1]. Allow me to respectfully disagree. His $5 billion investment in Goldman Sachs at the height of the crisis in 2008 has made him rather a lot of money[2]. Something of a contradiction for someone so outspokenly suspicious of derivative products. There were two sides to this investment: perpetual preferred shares paying a dividend of 10%, and warrants. Goldman bought back the shares in 2011 including a 10% early repayment bonus, meaning that Mr Buffett received three years of dividends plus 10%, totalling close to $2 billion. The warrants were issued at a strike price of $115 and exercised in March 2013, when shares were trading at around $159: another profit of $2 billion. There is no disputing Mr Buffett's talent, and the confidence signal his move sent investors worldwide should not be underestimated. However, the intrinsic value of a financial innovation does

---

[1] Berkshire Hathaway Annual Report 2012.
[2] "Buffett to Invest $5 billion in Goldman", *Wall Street Journal*, 24/09/2008.

not depend on whether Berkshire Hathaway profits from it[3]. Berkshire opted for a portfolio of derivatives because the risk/reward ratio was particularly attractive at that moment and these products were appropriate considering the objective.

We cannot really question the progress enabled by innovations in financial engineering over the last century, progress that has found its way to us, citizens and consumers of the 21st century. Advances of such magnitude would have been unattainable without unprecedented levels of capital and risk mutualisation. The issue of control remains, of course, but isn't that always true of significant innovations?

The aim of this book is to shed (some) light on the financial markets and objectively introduce a few key principles. I have been a trader for 20 years, and I still feel frustrated at the paucity of information available in the media on my job and that of my peers. Having published a first book on arbitrage[4], I decided to attempt an introduction to modern finance that I hope will be different in its approach, simplicity and appreciation of what people actually want to know. Maybe by explaining things clearly we can deconstruct and remove the myth surrounding the essentially straightforward financial innovations that have allowed us to fundamentally meet the challenges of our time.

That will be the common thread as we move through the book: starting from easily accessible examples, I hope to take you on a journey towards something bigger – building on or adding to existing knowledge so you can tackle the issues that require more complex (albeit well within the grasp of most people) solutions.

When I use the term finance, I mean capital market finance, and I will focus specifically on the complex products known as derivatives. Rather than describing these products in detail, I want to stick to their underlying

---

[3] And what about the investment in Goldman Sachs itself, a bank that trades extensively in derivatives for its own account and that of its clients? At the time of the 2012 Annual Report, Berkshire no longer held Goldman's preferred shares but still had the warrants in its portfolio.
[4] "The Complete Arbitrage Deskbook", McGraw-Hill Professional Publishing, 2000.

principles, just like an engineer who could explain how a steam engine works, but not its myriad applications.

Since my market background is primarily in shares, you will have to excuse a certain bias towards this particular asset class. It is probably for the best though: it is relatively easy to follow the price of a stock and to understand how the market is structured to facilitate transactions, especially because shares today are mostly traded transparently and electronically. Automation and transparency are not always as established for bonds, commodities and currencies.

This book proposes to explore the fundamentals while respecting simple guidelines:

- No unnecessary display of complexity: there is plenty of detailed information and sophisticated models out there for readers with, or aspiring to, a more technical expertise. My target audience is neither; you just need to know what shares, bonds and currencies are so I can examine slightly more abstract notions.
- A minimum amount of mathematics: I had to include some, but the major ideas require no complex formula.
- Simple, clear explanations, and concrete examples.
- 15 fundamental principles: no more, no less. That may sound like a lot, but each one is covered in only 10 pages.
- All chapters start with the same question: "What are we talking about?" and end with "Why it matters". My job is to tell you where we are going and make sure you arrive safely!

If I do my job properly, you will accompany me on a journey of intellectual discovery, with no yawning! Naturally, the techniques and strategies that result from these principles keep thousands of statistics PhDs busy the world over, but we can still approach these issues in a straightforward manner. Care to try?

Here are the 15 principles we will cover:

- The world's oldest couple: risk/return
- Trading on chance
- Time is money: interest rates
- Valuation and mark-to-market
- Spot trading and deferred delivery
- Short-selling
- Cash and derivatives
- Risk measurement and management
- Collateralisation
- Over-the-counter and listed products
- Indexation
- Asset management and proprietary trading
- Financing and refinancing
- Optionality
- Delta hedging

Obviously, it would be easy to find a trader or banker who would claim that my choices are arbitrary, simplistic and lack depth. Equally, I might be accused of dumbing down. This is all fair enough; I am fine with it. I make no claim to be exhaustive and have no intention of describing the inner workings of a trading floor. Nor is it my intention to justify anybody's behaviour. If you finish this book without getting bored and having actually learned something, it will be job well done.

I.   The World's Oldest Couple: Risk/Return

1.   What are we talking about?

Many of us are firm believers in the old maxims "nothing ventured, nothing gained" and "no guts, no glory": the idea being that a gain – whether tangible such as a large sum of money or intangible such as acclaim – requires taking risk.

Trading embodies this adage and this way of thinking. All traders operate in an environment where risk is omnipresent and profits are very strongly correlated to the risk actually taken, i.e. not hedged[5]. More and more risks can be exchanged by constantly evolving financial instruments, but the basic problem remains: if I hedge a risk, it is transferred to someone else. Who? At what price? What is the cumulative effect for the economy? To address these issues, quantitative finance has an extensive range of models, often in the form of partial derivatives, and we will touch upon these later.

But for now, we cannot avoid needing the help of statistics 101.

2.   Small stats refresher (don't worry, it'll be fine!)

Consider a situation in which an event can have only two outcomes, denoted A and B – for example a coin toss. If only two events can occur, their probability P_A and P_B are complementary, i.e. their sum is equal to 1:

$$P_A + P_B = 1$$

This means that B is certain if A does not occur, and vice versa. The analogy with a coin toss is straightforward: $P_A = P_B = 0.5 = 50\%$.

---

[5] A risk is hedged for a given portfolio if the value of this portfolio is unaffected by a manifestation of that risk, i.e. a change in certain specifically identified parameters.

Suppose that the occurrence of A results in a gain G_A and that of B in a gain G_B. G_A and G_B can be negative for a loss. The *expected gain* EG for the event is calculated as follows:

$$EG = P_A \times G_A + P_B \times G_B$$

The term *expected* indicates an average, which corresponds to the following statement: if the event occurred a large number of times, on *average* the gain or loss would be equal to EG.

In the case of the coin toss, $P_A = P_B = 0.5$ (a one in two chance). If we attribute a gain $G_A = \$1$ to a heads flip and a loss $G_B = -\$1$ to a tails flip, $EG = 0.5 \times \$1 + 0.5 \times (-\$1) = \$0$, i.e. exactly what you might think: with as many chances of winning \$1 as losing \$1, on average we can expect nothing. To be very clear on the notion of expectation, let us reiterate the point: if you play once, there will be a gain or loss of \$1. But if you play a large number of times, you will find that you have not gained or lost anything in the end.

We can easily extend this reasoning to any situation in which a random event can lead only to situations which are mutually exclusive (cannot take place at the same time) and have a finite number (rolling a die, or picking a number or colour on a roulette wheel, etc.).

In practice, the difficulty with this formula lies in the calculation of P_A and P_B, often based on enumerating outcomes. By contrast, G_A and G_B are generally simpler to assess. For example, the probability of getting heads on the toss of a coin is 1-in-2 or 50%, while the probability of getting a 1 on a roll of a six-sided, non-loaded die is 1-in-6 or about 16.67%. There are however more complex situations (the lottery for example, with its multitude of winning combinations, see below), making calculations significantly more difficult.

3.   Heads or tails?

"If only I could win the lottery!" Everybody at some point has stared at their lottery ticket and fantasised about the golden beaches of the Bahamas! The lottery is an extreme manifestation of the risk-return couple: if you win, you win big; everyone else has paid only a modest amount.

For the purpose of the exercise, let us consider two situations. First, the purchase of a lottery ticket. Second, a friend offers you the following bet: you choose heads or tails, he flips the coin three times, and if it lands on the side you chose at least twice, you win $5; otherwise, you owe him $10. What on earth do you do?

In both cases (lottery and bet), a similar question comes to mind: what risk should you take for what expected gain? The lottery is an upfront loss (the purchase of the ticket) in exchange for a possible future gain, while the coin flip is a subsequent loss or gain. The only difference is that the lottery administrator (in most countries this is a state-run business) requires a participation fee to access the draw, and these fees will constitute the prize pool for the winners. The ticket, bought before the event, is nothing more than an option, in other words the right to participate in the draw, which is itself totally random. Frankly, intuition is of little use in these situations, as we can prove with a quick statistical calculation. Let's start with the lottery.

You choose a line of five numbers between 1 and 49, and if the numbers drawn correspond to the ones you have chosen, you win the jackpot. Repetitions are not allowed and the order does not matter: you are assured of the jackpot if the five numbers drawn at random are the ones you have chosen. The universe of possibilities is the total number of combinations of five numbers from the 49 that go into the draw. This number is well known in number theory and is equal to $C(49, 5) = 49! / (5! \times 44!) = 1,906,884$[6]. So if you play one line of five numbers, the probability of winning the jackpot is therefore 1 in 1,906,884. Not great, is it?

Is it worth playing? If we apply what we have already learned, the expected gain can be easily calculated: it is equal to the probability of winning (P_+) times the gain (G_+), plus the probability of losing (P_-) times the loss (G_-):

---

[6] "n !", or *n factorial*, is the product of all integers between 1 and n: $5! = 1 \times 2 \times 3 \times 4 \times 5 = 120$, $10! = 1 \times 2 \times 3 \times 4 \times 5 \times 6 \times 7 \times 8 \times 9 \times 10 = 3,628,800$.

$$EG = P_+ \times G_+ + P_- \times G_-$$

where:

- G_- = cost of the ticket, say $5
- P_- = probability of losing = 1,906,883/1,906,884 = 0.999999476
- P_+ = probability of winning = 1/1,906,884 = 0.000000524
- G_+ = the jackpot, say $2,000,000

So: EG = $2,000,000 × 1/1,906,884 - $5 × 1,906,883/1,906,884 ≈ -$3.95.

You might as well put $4 straight in to the organiser's pocket. Incidentally, a small additional step makes it possible to calculate the expected gain above which it becomes reasonable to invest $5: EG turns positive if and only if G+ ≥ $5 × 1,906,883 = $9,534,415. In other words, the jackpot has to be $9.5 million for the expected gain to be positive, i.e. to have a chance of winning, *on average*.

In practice, however, no one plays on average; even a highly motivated person could not buy enough tickets to genuinely and significantly increase their chances. Nevertheless, the average calculation is perfectly applicable for the lottery organiser: if 1,906,884 different lines have been entered, it knows it will have to write someone out a cheque for $2 million. Its risk is the players' opportunity, and vice versa. However, if the lottery is profitable in the long run, and we know it is, it means that, whichever way you look at it, the expected gain for the players is negative.

So, the "play or don't play" decision tree is as follows:
- For $5 and one line, you could win the jackpot.
- However, since the expected gain is negative, you essentially enter into a bet in which you are *almost* certain to lose money, and if you had bought *all* the tickets you would be *certain* to.

It is therefore up to each person to decide how likely they are to win right away in a process statistically constructed so that players pay out more than they receive. Even though the real statistical calculations are much more complex because of all the different lottery forms (additional numbers, bonus balls, multiple draws, reusable lines, etc.), the conclusion is basically the same: it takes an unwavering faith in the universe to play the lottery.

For our friend's challenge, the calculation is slightly different. Once we consider all the different outcomes, you have a 50/50 chance of winning[7]:

- $G_+ = \$5$
- $G_- = -\$10$
- $P_+ = 0.5$
- $P_- = 0.5$

Therefore, $EG = 0.5 \times \$5 + 0.5 \times (-\$10) = -\$2.5$. To further illustrate what is meant by expected gain, this result can be interpreted as follows: if you decide to accept your friend's challenge once, you will win \$5 or lose \$10. However, if you played the challenge many times, you could expect to lose \$2.5. The decision on whether to accept the challenge is still yours, but at least you can now make an informed choice.

4. The price of risk

To illustrate another concept following on from what we have already learned, let us consider a slightly more complex situation in which the number of possible outcomes is much greater. A die has n faces and is manufactured in such a way that, in 100 rolls, each face i appears P_i times on average, without all the P_is necessarily being equal. Each outcome has a probability $(P_i / 100)$ and leads to a gain G_i (which can be negative, i.e. a loss).

---

[7] On the first toss, the likelihood of (H)eads/(T)ails is 50/50 because both outcomes have an equal chance of materialising. On the second toss, there are four possibilities for the two combined tosses: H/H, H/T, T/H, T/T, each with a 25% chance of materialising. On the third toss, there are 8 possibilities: H/H/H, H/H/T, H/T/H, H/T/T, T/H/H, T/H/T, T/T/H, T/T/T, each with a 12.5% (= 1/8) chance of occurring. There are 4 possibilities with 2 or 3 Hs and 4 possibilities with 2 or 3 Ts, therefore a 50/50 chance overall.

The expected gain for the player who decides to roll this die is calculated in the same way as in the coin problem:

$$EG = P_1 \times G_1 + P_2 \times G_2 + P_3 \times G_3 + \ldots + P_n \times G_n$$

But how variable is the result from one game to another? If we take the case of two outcomes – a gain of $5 and a loss of $1 – there is a significant dispersion between them. When the number of outcomes increases, it is useful to make this dispersion tangible. In statistics, this is represented by a quantity called *standard deviation*:

$$\sigma G = \sqrt{(P_1 \times G_1^2 + P_2 \times G_2^2 + P_3 \times G_3^2 + \cdots + P_n \times G_n^2) - EG^2}$$

In the case of a game with 2 outcomes (+ $5 and -$1), EG = $2 and the standard deviation is equal to:

$$\sigma G = \sqrt{0,5 \times 5^2 + 0,5 \times (-1)^2 - (2)^2} = 3$$

Intuitively, this figure is the distance from each of the two results: +$5 and -$1 are separated by 6 points, 3 on either side of a statistical middle (which happens to be EG).

How can we use standard deviation? Suppose that a game of chance presents you with a choice of two scenarios: in both cases, a random event takes place, there is a very large number of outcomes and you are given only two pieces of information: the expected gain and the standard deviation (for example, you are presented with 2 dice, each with a large number of faces). What is the best choice? A roll with an expected gain of $150 but a standard deviation of $300, or a roll with an expected gain of $100, but a standard deviation of $20? The second alternative seems better because the dispersion of the possible results is less: if you generally fall between $80 and $120, it is better than generally falling between -$150 and $450.

By comparing the expectation and standard deviation, we can deduce the cost of risk: in the first case, each $1 of gain is accompanied by $2 of uncertainty (= $300/$150). In the second case, each $1 gain is accompanied by $0.20 of uncertainty (= $20/$100). In practice, the expectation/standard deviation ratio is used because it has the advantage of growing with the desirability of the situation: a ratio of 5 ($100/$20) is much more desirable than a ratio of 0.5 ($150/$300)[8]. This is the essence of the famous Sharpe ratio, which is very often used in the analysis of various investments and their respective attractiveness. Alternative measures have been proposed over time, but the Sharpe ratio has the advantage of being simple and well established.

Let us be very clear: each of the above scenarios can result in good or bad surprises. You might gain on the first and lose on the second, despite the examples given. Everything depends on the *distribution of outcomes*, i.e. the frequency with which each of the values occurs. Expectation and standard deviation capture only behaviour on average, as opposed to a single roll of the die or just a small number of rolls. In the real world, on the financial markets, no one knows the distribution of returns of financial assets, but we can estimate their expectation and standard deviation. The choice of one instrument over another is therefore exactly the same choice as our two scenarios: the Sharpe ratio sheds light on things and can help you make your mind up.

This can also be extended to market operators. What is a trader after all? A living, breathing apparatus capable of making investment or trading decisions with a positive expectation: at any given moment, several events are likely to occur, but the trader manages their position in such a way that the losses resulting from negative outcomes are lower than the gains generated by positive ones. They are therefore a human decision tree facing a random series, with each of their decisions comparable to a dice roll or a coin toss that will result in a loss or profit once the market has had its say. For every $1 a trader manages, they make a return day after day with an average and a variance; in other words, they can be characterised by a Sharpe ratio. So the simple things we have learned would allow us to quickly compare two traders, or more accurately their investment processes, to determine which one offers the most attractive cost of risk.

---

[8] This ratio is dimensionless: EG is homogeneous to an amount in cash, as is σG. So we are dividing apples by apples.

5.   Risk tolerance and utility function

Let us go back to the example of your friend, who is really keen to toss his coin, only this time on simpler terms. Heads, you win $5; tails you lose $1. The expected gain (0.5 x $5 – 0.5 x $1 = $2) is largely in your favour, even if the risk of losing is real. You decide to go for it and win a handsome $5 thanks to the wonder of statistics.

But your friend is an avid gambler and wants to make up for his loss. The *modus operandi* remains the same, but the gain is now $500 and the loss $100. Or maybe he really ups the ante: $5,000 of gain for $1,000 of loss. The prize is tempting...but, on the other hand, can you afford to lose $1,000 on a coin toss? It's a lot of money, and you may have it earmarked for a purchase or want to put it aside for a rainy day.

This very simple example highlights the notion of risk tolerance. Faced with the same statistical probability (50/50 in all cases), each individual will react differently. Even if the expected gain is positive, each person's temperament, financial situation and impulsiveness will be a factor in deciding whether to take this risk. Mathematically, it is indisputable that the rational choice is to take the bet because its expected gain is significantly positive. The thing is, we are not all unconditionally rational.

In this case, some (maybe even many) people will focus on the big loss, not the expected gain. Everyone makes a personal risk assessment and makes their decision accordingly. In economic terms, each individual (or group of individuals) has a "utility function", i.e. their own barometer of what a risk represents and how much fear it generates.

The notion of probability depends on risk appetite. This is rather counter-intuitive since we would like probability to depend on the conditions under which an event occurs, on a formal model, rather than on the characteristics of the observer. It is in fact a fundamental element of modern statistical calculations and financial modelling: the world is seen as a place where probability is dependent on risk appetite, even if in many cases the assumption of a "risk neutral" probability is held true, i.e. an operator has no prior bias or sensitivity to risk. The word 'prior' is essential here because what makes the decision difficult – the possibility of a significant loss – pre-exists the bet and the choice that must be taken. Put differently, a risk-neutral operator assesses only the risk induced by the proposed transaction, not any other. For example, the decision is not affected by their current financial situation. On the other hand, they are at least solvent. If losing $1,000 bankrupts you because you would not be able to pay that debt, the bet takes on a completely different meaning. Is it realistic to assume a risk-neutral world? Probably not. Consequently, academic research has long wandered into the territory of behavioural finance, which places risk appetite at its very core.

The lottery exploits the same phenomenon of risk aversion, but in the opposite direction: the lure of a colossal gain totally obscures the tiny probability of actually obtaining it. We can also rely on the organiser to bombard us with the stories of gleeful winners and how easy it all was.

6.   Why it matters

The risk/return profile is the cornerstone of decision-making on a trading floor. Any trading decision can be reduced to an analysis of expected gain and standard deviation.

But shedding light on the risk/return dichotomy presupposes that it has been constructed:

- from the notion of probability, which is the only reasonably effective tool for evaluating randomness;
- from the definition of expected gain, which makes it possible to evaluate a random process by making a distinction between what happens in a one-off scenario (one roll of the dice) and what happens on average (many rolls of the dice);
- from the cost of risk, expressed in a measurable form (for example, by a Sharpe ratio);
- and from the notion of risk aversion, embodied in everyone's utility function.

Financial theorists today have no choice but to return to these fundamentals. In the presence of unpredictable random phenomena such as prices of financial instruments (see next chapter), the reality could not be simpler: only a rigorous mathematical approach can lead to as rational a decision as possible.

II.   Trading on chance

1.   What are we talking about?

All this is well and good, but we would know about it if operators on the trading floor spent their time tossing coins. And yet...

Take for example the case of a listed stock: its evolution is perfectly random and similar in essence to the tossing of a coin, albeit one with a very large number of faces, each of them likely to appear with a probability that we do not know and that varies in time. The behaviour of economic actors is certainly rational: the CEO of a listed company must have a vision for the future and a strategy to best grow his company's profits; similarly, individual and institutional investors would purchase this stock only after rigorous and conclusive analysis. Price formation mechanisms are no more random or arbitrary: supply and demand are real; many perfectly determined transactions are recorded every day for significant volumes, but the price resulting from these transactions is nonetheless a manifestation of chance. It cannot be predicted with certainty from one moment to the next. Each investor may have a prior idea of what they should buy or sell, but they are all hostage to the performance of the market. This is true of shares and all other financial assets: bonds, currencies, oil, etc.

A great deal of research has been done on the subject, and the conclusion is irrefutable: nothing can predict the price of a stock with a degree of certainty that would make a gain easily achievable. First, the probability of being right or wrong is 50/50 since a price can only increase or decrease. As a result of various assumptions or calculations, you can, at any given moment, convince yourself that this probability is swinging towards a rise (or a fall), and make a profit based on this conviction. But what way will it swing next? On average, in the statistical sense of expectation, there is no procedure enabling you to calculate an exploitable probability and make a profit from it[9].

---

[9] At the risk of repeating myself, it is possible at any moment to bet on an increase or decrease, to be right and consequently to make money. But the probability of being

Although the price of a share is random, there are ways to analyse it. At this point, we need to distinguish between two very different approaches:

- Financial analysts will use available financial statements – balance sheet, income statement and presentations from management – to get educated on the company's operational performance. From there, they will determine a "theoretical" price for now and the future. They can see in advance whether the quoted price is significantly different from this theoretical valuation and deduce from that whether to buy, sell or stay away.
- Traders operate completely differently: they might make a note of a gap between the quoted price and the theoretical price (based on their own financial analysis), but the most important thing to them is how the security behaves over time, depending on the aggregate supply and demand curves.

Plotting the price of a stock over time, we get the significantly jerky curves typical of a random and fractal time series. Let us look at the share price of Total over 10 years and over 1 day (Figures 2.1 and 2.2).

---

right *several times in a row,* a must if you want to make money continually, is extremely low and decreases with time.

Figure 2.1 - *Total closing price over 10 years*

Source: Bloomberg.

Figure 2.2 - *Total share price on 02/03/2017*

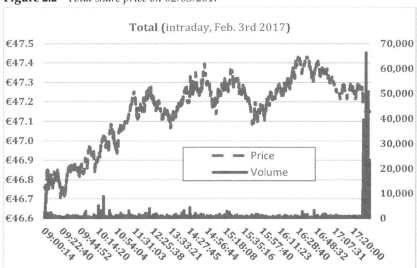

The bars on the far right represent trades from the closing auction at 17:35, which always attracts very high liquidity.
Source: Bloomberg.

At any scale, the shapes are similar, and the reason is that the path is random and continuous, whatever the time scale. Rather than an ability to analyse a result or question an executive to make them say something they do not want to, being a trader is about the statistics of random variables. This branch of mathematics is called stochastic calculus.

Faced with this situation, the response of practitioners has been relatively simple: since an exact calculation is not possible, we have to make do with an approximation. In the mathematical world of random distributions, one seems to get it about right and has the enormous advantage of being mathematically sympathetic (i.e. very well understood): normal distribution. Adopting this approximation, we can conclude that many financial variables have a yield that can be described by a normal distribution; in other words, prices have a lognormal[10] distribution.

What is meant by "follow a normal distribution"? Quite simply, the probability of a certain price variation from one period to another[11] can be obtained by referring to a known formula, which is found in other random phenomena and which commonly takes the form of a bell curve (Figure 2.3).

---

[10] In quantitative finance, yield is defined as $r_t = \ln (P_t/P_{t-1})$, where P_t = price at period t, P_{t-1} = price at the previous period t - 1, and ln () = natural logarithm. If the yield is normal, the price is lognormal.

[11] Generally, a period is a day, but it could be any time interval, for example a few minutes or a few hours.

Figure 2.3 - *Bell curves representative of a normal distribution*

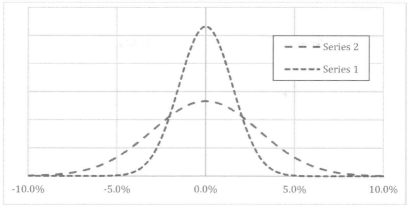

For each possible future movement (the horizontal axis represents the yield of the next period, ranging here from -10 % to +10 %), we can assign a probability (the vertical axis, left blank here to keep things simple). The further away from the centre, the lower the probability. Simply put, it is highly probable that a normal variable will change very little from its current value (centre of the curve), and highly improbable that it will change considerably (far left and far right of the curve).

A normal distribution depends on just two quantities: mean (or expectation) and standard deviation. For example, the two curves above have an equal mean (0, the curves are centred on the vertical axis) but a different standard deviation (series 1 has a lower standard deviation than series 2 - the achievable values are less scattered).

Each of these curves could represent the observed, and by extension the expected, return of a stock. To draw a parallel with the previous chapter, the stock is like a die with a very large number of faces, with each roll determining the price from one period to the next, and for which we can quantify only an expected gain (the mean) and a standard deviation.

Of course, we do have access to the mean and standard deviation after the event. For example, by looking at the prices of a stock over a year, it is easy to calculate an average return and a standard deviation. There is nothing to suggest that these values from a previous sample are the same as the true value of the mean and standard deviation, and there is no guarantee that the coming year will play out in exactly the same way as last year. Once we postulate knowing the distribution of a stock's return, does this knowledge create an opportunity for gain? Unfortunately not: normal distribution is strictly symmetrical, so at any given moment the chances of benefiting from a rise are equal to those of benefiting from a fall.

All of this would be very useful from a theoretical point of view, were it not plain wrong in practice. The distribution of Total's share returns and the closest possible bell curve are shown below (Figure 2.4).

Figure 2.4. - *Comparison of Total share returns and a normal distribution*

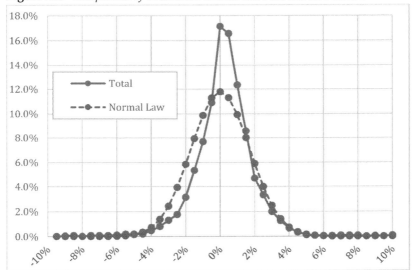

NB: This curve shows, for each variation in Total (x-axis), the frequency of this value over a 10-year track record. For example, a daily variation around 0 is found in about 17% of the daily data over 10 years. A variation of about -2% is found in just over 3% of cases.

Ouch, not exactly a perfect match, is it? What we can see is that the actual distribution is *leptokurtic*. This barbaric word means that the distribution is more heavily concentrated about the mean – let us take a closer look (Figures 2.5 and 2.6).

Figure 2.5. - *Distribution of Total's returns compared with a normal distribution (lower tail)*

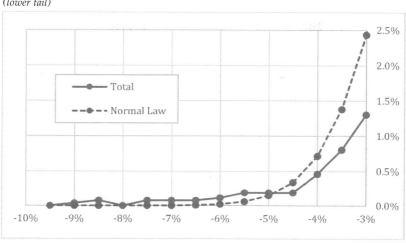

Figure 2.6 - *Distribution of Total's returns compared with a normal distribution (upper tail)*

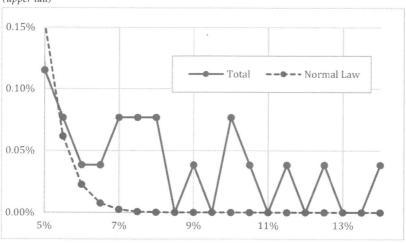

This is the nightmare for any professional or amateur trader. Simply put, the "distribution tails" are too fat, which means that the probability of a catastrophic event is actually much higher than in the proposed model. This is apparent in the graphs above, where the blue lines corresponding to Total are above those corresponding to the normal distribution of identical mean and standard deviation. Why is this bad? Because a drop of 20% or 30% is a stock market crash, bringing about the consequences with which we are all too familiar, and occurs in real life much more often than normal modelling would suggest. The same can be said of market spikes, although it is less intuitive. A portfolio of derivatives in a large financial institution is often delta-hedged, i.e. immune to moderate movements (see Chapter 15 on delta management). A bullish shock, which would come as a pleasant surprise to a passive holder, can cause substantial losses on a portfolio of this type. In reality, everyone prefers a rise to a fall, but above all a regulated market, i.e. gradual changes rather than sudden shocks.

All this can be summarised as follows:

- It is impossible to anticipate the behaviour of a financial asset because its movement is essentially random.
- And when one tries by using reasonable mathematical modelling, the risks of extreme outcomes are chronically underestimated, giving a false sense of security. In particular, this sense manifests itself in a natural, but totally erroneous, tendency to draw conclusions about future changes from the observation of past movements.

This means that all reasoning surrounding expected gains is distorted and all extreme risks are systematically underestimated. All hedging schemes designed to protect against these risks are therefore potentially inadequate and insufficient. To make matters worse, all this has been common knowledge for a long time.

The collapse of Lehman Brothers was, for example, a leptokurtic event, as were the 9/11 attacks and the sovereign debt crisis of 2008-2010. This is not to say that all negative events are unexpected and far-reaching, but it is important to recognise that extremes are so under-represented *in theory* that most simulations predict losses which are too low. In addition, one could argue that the effects of extreme outcomes are non-linear[12], so the more

---

[12] Non-linear means that losses resulting from a 10% decrease are potentially more than double losses resulting from a 5% decrease. This is particularly true, for example,

wrong the model is, the more severe the consequence of an unexpected shock.

This discussion leads to a rather pessimistic view of risk: what should we do to protect ourselves in an environment where the model itself is mistaken? There is no miracle cure. There is no such thing as zero risk, but losses can be mitigated. This is the whole point of Basel III banking regulation, which had three distinct aims:

- Make it harder for large financial institutions to take risks by forcing a more restrictive assessment of these risks. In particular, liquidity risk has come to the fore, having previously been undervalued or even overlooked.
- Impose a much larger capital cushion, especially for "systemic" institutions, i.e. institutions whose failure has a disproportionate impact on the economy. The general idea is that a market participant must be able to assume heavier and more realistic losses on its own regulatory capital in the light of historically observed crises.
- Limit contagion from one participant to another to avoid devastating domino effects.

Chapter 8 on risk management will present an algebraic vision of risk, which is the one commonly adopted and which unquestionably serves its purpose, albeit at the cost of approximations – the introduction of lognormal distribution – whose severe limitations should never be forgotten.

I would like to offer a final word on the relevance of the cost of risk as we have defined it. If we look back at the Total share over a year, we can establish an average return and calculate the standard deviation of daily returns. By taking the corresponding Sharpe ratio, i.e. the ratio between mean and standard deviation, we obtain the cost of risk for this security. The previous question is still relevant: should we choose a security whose observed (daily) yield is 0.35% with a standard deviation of 0.9% (Sharpe ratio of 0.39), or one with an average yield of 0.5% and a standard deviation

---

of an optional position whose gamma captures the variation as the square of the market variation; see Chapters 14 on optionality and 15 on delta hedging.

of 0.6% (Sharpe ratio of 0.62)? In reality, this question only makes sense if we assume that past performance is indicative of future returns, which is a misunderstanding of the random nature of the phenomena in question. We can therefore say that if the Sharpe ratio is used as a basis for investment decisions, this must be done in an informed manner, i.e. with awareness of the underlying assumptions.

2. Why it matters

Here are the main issues of market finance:
- The market is dominated by structural random behaviour that cannot be rigorously modelled.
- So far, theories tend to underestimate extremes, resulting in huge losses when these extremes occur, especially because the losses are almost never linear in relation to market movements. However, the existing models are the best we have[13], and at least they enable mathematically correct risk analyses.
- In the case of financial assets or trading strategies, the analysis of randomness usually involves estimating an expected return (the equivalent of a mean) and a standard deviation (volatility, which *de facto* represents a risk), despite all the widely known reservations, as I have explained.

These ideas provide the basis for a quantitative analysis of financial markets. Financial engineers have subsequently used them to model increasingly complex products, but sadly they have overestimated their control of risk.

---

[13] I should point out here that more refined distributions than normal distributions have been postulated, including some that incorporate random upward and downward shocks. The manipulation of these distributions is mathematically and numerically complex, which essentially means that the calculations are very long. Because of this, their use is far from being widespread.

III.   Time is money: interest rates

1.   What are we talking about?

You certainly have enterprising friends, don't you? Now one of them is asking you to bail them out by lending them $1,000 for a few weeks. Before you give your response, you have to ask yourself two questions. What chance is there that this money will never be repaid? Apart from the fact this person is a friend and you would therefore lend them money in a heartbeat, what remuneration would you need to take this risk?

Make no mistake, no one can answer these questions rigorously. We can model extensively, but credit risk assessment, with rare exceptions[14], is *exceedingly* difficult. The real estate and financial crisis of 2008 is yet again a perfect illustration.

Having said that, we can use a risk/return analysis to help study this little problem. Let us assume the following:
- p is the probability of default, i.e. the probability that the loan will not be repaid when it matures. If p = 20%, there is a 4-in-5 chance that the loan will be repaid in full.
- R is the recovery rate, i.e. the portion of the loan recovered in the event of default: 0% in a complete default, a bit higher if assets can be seized and sold. If R = 30 %, you get $300 back from the initial $1,000.
- r is the interest rate on the loan.

The expected gain from the operation is still:

$$EG = P_+ \times G_+ + P_- \times G_-$$

where (for a $1,000 loan):

---

[14] These exceptions are essentially central banks, but not all of them. Even sovereign states can default; central banks offer the huge advantage that they print money so they cannot default. They also set the interest rates at which they intervene.

- G_- = loss due to non-repayment, i.e. $-(1 - R) \times \$1,000$
- P_- = probability of losing = p,
- P_+ = probability of being repaid = 1 - p,
- G_+ = gain in case of full repayment = $r \times \$1,000$

So:

$$EG = - p \times (1 - R) \times \$1,000 + (1 - p) \times r \times \$1,000$$

The first term represents the loss in the event of default with a probability p, the second the gain due to interest in the event of full repayment, with a probability 1 - p. Default and repayment are two mutually exclusive outcomes. The difficulties begin here. What is p? What is R? What would r have to be to justify the loan, i.e. make EG reasonably positive?

A first approach might be to consider that p and R can be deduced from a rigorous credit analysis and feedback on a large number of similar loans: what is the borrower's income, financial stability, existing debt level, etc.? A default usually leads to bankruptcy and court proceedings or *at least* collective bargaining between the borrower and the lender, so many occurrences have (probably) been documented. In a large number of cases, it is possible to get an idea of what the creditors can recover, on average. Of course, the less similar the default situation is to known precedents, the more uncertain the estimated value of R. But historical analysis does offer points of reference.

In this average-based approach, there is reason to the expectation: a single loan is either repaid or it is not. But what we are trying to do here is measure probabilities in advance, and this can be done accurately only over a large number of loans. In real life, of course, this is exactly what happens: banks can observe default rates on a large portfolio. Then r is fixed to make the transaction profitable for the lender, *on average*.

If for example p = 10 %, R = 30 %:
- in 10% of cases, the lender will not be repaid in full, resulting in a loss of $70: only $30 is recovered in the liquidation of the borrower's assets;

- in 90% of cases, the lender will be repaid in full, with a gain of r x $100.

The rate that justifies the loan makes EG positive; EG is positive if and only if:

$$r \geq \frac{p \times (1 - R)}{(1 - p)}$$

EG must therefore be greater than 7.78% in our example. Sure, but should it not be 10% to guarantee a higher profit? Why not 15%? Obviously, r increases with p (the more likely the default, the higher the lender's remuneration should be), but it also increases when R decreases since the lender recovers less and less. Figure 3.1 shows the minimum rate calculated where R = 30%.

Figure 3.1 - *Minimum interest rate as a function of the default probability (R = 30%)*

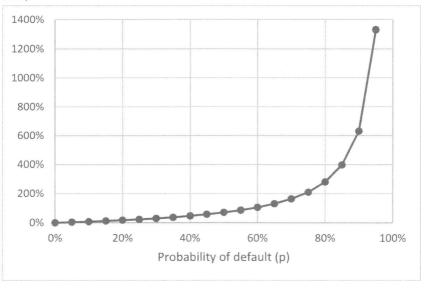

Figure 3.2 - *Minimum interest rate (probability of default up to 20%)*

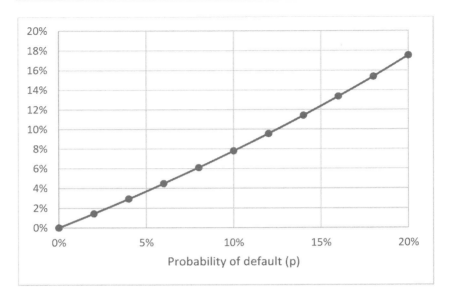

A default probability of 15% requires an interest rate of 12%; otherwise it is not worth the lender's while. Quite quickly, the rate becomes so high that it is impossible to accept unless you are desperate.

As we can see, the problem has not yet been fully resolved and the decision to lend (or not) is still not based on a totally satisfactory justification. Things get even more complicated if the borrower signs a promissory note entitling you to take a portion of their next wage packet as repayment. The loan is then secured – in financial terms we say "collateralised" – by an asset (in this case, a future wage packet). The guarantee reduces the risk, and therefore the interest rate, but by how much?

2. What are interest rates really made of?

If you look closely, an interest rate consists of four elements:
- a remuneration for the risk taken. Once the probability of default has been assessed, the equation above establishes a minimum rate;
- a commercial margin acceptable to everyone, i.e. an assessment by each party of the value of the service rendered;
- an element of compensation for monetary depreciation. All other things being equal, $1 today is not equivalent to $1 tomorrow, in a

month or in a year, regardless of any notion of lending or borrowing: inflation will have eroded its value. It is natural to expect the borrower to compensate the lender for this erosion;

- a refinancing cost. In real life, when a bank lends to one of its clients, it has to borrow a large part of that amount on the money markets. As a last resort, it will turn to its country's central bank if no one agrees to lend it the money. Between individuals, this cost also exists, but takes the form of an opportunity cost: the loaned money could have been bringing in interest if it had been in a savings account or invested elsewhere. It is this lost income that must be considered.

We can already discount one element: the commercial margin. For interbank transactions and capital markets, it does of course exist, but the formation of interest rates owes much more to the constraints imposed by the other three elements, so these are of greater interest to us. In other words, the commercial margin is by its very nature negotiable, and therefore arbitrary in time and space.

Inflation is published by official statistical institutes. It is calculated to measure baskets of current consumption (goods and services in proportions representative of everyone's life), i.e. it sticks very close to a pragmatic interpretation of inflation. This figure can therefore be used to serve our need to measure currency erosion. That leaves two elements: the price of the risk borne by the lender and the cost of (re)financing.

The cost of financing is also easily identifiable. Each institution knows that its own cost depends on the nature of its liabilities. Together with its customers' sight and term deposits, transactions with other commercial banks or with central banks form a combination whose cost is known. Although our initial problem has become somewhat simpler, we are unfortunately still struggling with the ultimate question: how do we assess and quantify the risk taken in a basic lending operation?

The answer is the same as the one given to the question of estimating the price of a share tomorrow, even knowing its price today: it is simply impossible. This cannot be repeated enough: it may be possible to make a one-off prediction about the behaviour of a stock and to make a profit. But it is impossible to keep making this prediction over time and be highly likely to make money on a consistent basis. The same applies to credit risk and, by extension, interest rates. We can estimate and model, but in the end what will happen tomorrow is in the lap of the gods.

The problem can be looked at in two ways, just like with the stock of a listed company. Financial analysts will focus on the income statement, strategy and operational efficiency. They will deduce a theoretical price of the shares and will position themselves in relation to this price. Traders observe the market price, and may even draw conclusions about the estimated performance of the company, but above all they will try to protect themselves against the price movements they know to be random. The same applies to credit risk: financial analysts will analyse the balance sheet, recurring cash flows and existing debt and can convince themselves that a loan has a good chance of being repaid. As a result, they can express a probability of default or a relevant interest rate in their research. This is exactly what rating agencies do. Using methodical analysis and monitoring over time, they are able – in theory – to assign a rating to a large number of borrowers with the following constraint: two borrowers with the same rating must by their nature carry the same probability of default and therefore pay the same interest rate. Using a rating agency is like buying its analysis methodology. Traders, on the other hand, observe the actual transactions between market participants and focus primarily on the movements in the random rates from one day to the next, against which they must hedge their portfolios.

However, there are two important differences between equities and interest rates.

- The first is the *size* of their respective markets. The fixed income market is much bigger than the equities market because it encompasses all forms of lending, borrowing and credit risk, whatever the parties involved. Whether it is government debt, a mortgage or a consumer loan for a vehicle, the transaction is governed by an interest rate that represents how the borrower pays the lender. The debt itself can take various forms: typically a financial instrument, such as a bond, or a contract such as a real estate loan, a promissory note, etc.

- The second difference is the *structure* of the market: monetary policy is managed by a higher institution, the central bank. In addition to its role as "lender of last resort", the central bank's function is to regulate the circulation and cost of money, usually with targets for economic aggregates such as inflation. The presence of an agent that does what it deems necessary to regulate the fixed income market is a major guarantee for the financial system since there is absolute security as a last resort. However, it is only accessible to certain regulated institutions and under certain conditions. The bankruptcy of Lehman Brothers further clarified the conditions under which this liquidity of last resort could be used.

Despite these differences, the general idea is the same: in the battle of chance against mathematical modelling, chance wins hands down and it should not be forgotten, despite there being some very useful tools out there.

3. The notion of term structure

All of the above neglects the duration of the loan: obviously, lending money over 1 month does not present the same risk as lending over 1 year, even if the borrower is the same. Accordingly, the interest rate increases with the maturity of the operation, as shown in Figure 3.3.

Figure 3.3 - *Interest rates by currency and maturity*

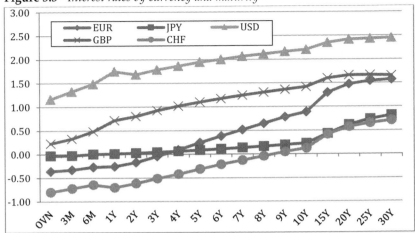

There is no point showing an interest rate without specifying *who* the borrower is. These are the interbank rates, i.e. the rates offered between major international financial institutions. EUR = euro, USD = US dollar, JPY = yen, CHF = Swiss franc, GBP = Pound sterling.
Source: Bloomberg, 22 September 2017.

So, everything we have already learned is made more complex by an additional dimension that is not present with stocks: the maturity. The *term structure* is highly correlated: the 3-month rate is unlikely to move without the 2-month and 4-month rates also being affected. On the other hand, there is little correlation between a 3-month rate and a 10-year rate or a 30-year rate. For this reason, fixed income trading teams are often split in two, so one group can deal with the short term and the other with the long term. The two jobs are different.

4. Collateralisation and interest rates

It is only natural to think about taking a guarantee when lending money. Whether you are dealing with a private individual borrower, a large industrial group or a government, any reasonable lender would want a guarantee on all or part of its loan.

In capital market finance, the guarantee is often provided in the form of "collateral", i.e. a financial asset delivered to the lender which they hold until the debt is repaid, and with which they can do as they please in the event of default.

What assets do traders have at their disposal to obtain a loan? Essentially, the positions they have taken out while conducting their normal business, generally shares or bonds. So any trader can offer up the assets they hold as collateral if they wish to borrow. This is called refinancing. The assets were first financed when they were purchased. Putting them up as collateral makes it possible to recover an equivalent amount in the form of credit.

Is the interest rate of a collateralised, or secured, transaction the same as that of a loan between the same participants without collateral? Of course not: the risk is not the same, so the remuneration of the transaction should not be the same. A secured loan costs less than the same loan without collateral. Indeed, the absence of any collateral makes some transactions impossible. A mortgage, for example, is relatively easy to negotiate when the property is pledged to the lending bank. It is pretty obvious that the outcome would not be the same without that pledge.

So what is the interest rate worth in the presence of collateral? Just like the credit risk assessment for a simple loan, this is another question to which there is no exact answer. What we *can* say is that this rate is worth whatever the two parties are willing to agree to. However, there are objective elements of assessment, such as the quality of the collateral, the financial soundness of the borrower and the duration of the loan. For example, collateral in the form of US Treasury bonds has more value than the shares of a small regional company in Arkansas. But it's not an exact science.

I can tell what you're thinking: is there *really* such a thing as a risk-free interest rate? There are two possible answers to that question:
- In the case of a secured loan, the risk is obviously very low if the value of the collateral far exceeds that of the loan. This is why property transactions require a deposit, although the regularity of property crises shows that the system is far from infallible.
- Unsecured debt is more interesting. The logical conclusion based on what we have learned is that the only truly solvent borrower is the central bank of a country with a reasonably developed

economy. The reason is simple: the central bank can print money, so it is always able to repay its debt. The creation of additional money will of course have immediate consequences on the value of that money because of the inevitable inflation, but creditors know they will be repaid. In practice this never happens because the role of a central bank is not to borrow, but to lend (which also increases the money supply). As the central banks in modern economies are politically independent, it removes the temptation of governments to finance their election pledges with new debt that could have a devastating inflationary effect.

The economic agent that most closely resembles a risk-free creditor, and can therefore borrow at a risk-free rate, is not the central bank, but the government of a country with a reasonably developed and stable economy. The qualification "reasonably developed" should be seen not as an arbitrary judgement, but a factual assessment: an economy where the fundamental mechanisms are more or less respected, i.e. whose prices, flows and agents are not arbitrarily controlled and/or directed by public authorities.

For each of the major currencies, there is therefore a benchmark where the cost of borrowing brings about a risk-free rate. For example, the US sovereign debt yield sets the tone for the US dollar, the British debt yield does the same on the pound, and so on. The euro is a bit different because the eurozone is made up of countries with developed but disparate economies. French financial institutions consider that their risk-free rate is that of French debt, while Italians typically use Italian Treasury yields. This is a fairly simple principle that can be applied as a general rule.

5. Discounting and accrual

It has all been a bit theoretical so far, so now for something concrete. Suppose a company sells one of its products for payment in 30 days. Intuitively, we would be more confident of receiving $1 today than in 30 days. It is still possible that the client could go bankrupt within the next 30 days and not be able to pay its debt.

The natural question is then: what is the *present* value of this future cash flow? In concrete terms, if the company contacted a bank and presented it with this situation, how much would the bank lend today?

Now let us suppose that Airbus has sold an A320 for $50 million, to be paid within 6 months. Since it needs money right now to finalise delivery of the aircraft, Airbus goes to a bank with the sales contract, signed by a reputable buyer whose solvency is not in question. After having calculated an interest rate on this transaction – say 4%– the bank will lend Airbus the amount M as follows:

$$M = \frac{\$50,000,000}{1 + 4\,\% \times \left(^6/_{12}\right)} = \$49,019,607.84\ \$$$

Why? Because this amount matches present and future flows:
- Today, Airbus receives $49,019,608.
- In 6 months, the sale is concluded. Airbus receives $50 million from the buyer, and must repay the bank the principal ($49,019,608) plus interest, which ran at 4% over 6 months, or $49,019,607.84 x 4% x (6/12) = $980,392.16. The sum of the two ($49,019,607.84 $ + $980,392.16) is equal to $50 million, so all the money from the sale is paid to the bank to extinguish the debt.

This type of calculation is called *discounting*. What are the important parameters? Basically, the interest rate. How is it fixed? Surprise, surprise: by the level of risk associated with the flow. How can I work this out? By studying the credit of the borrower – Airbus here or someone similar – and assuming that what happened in the past will happen again now. It is the bank's responsibility to carry out this analysis and to propose a rate that remunerates its risk – including a margin, of course. For its part, Airbus can consult several institutions and have them compete for this transaction.

Discounting is a fairly simple mechanism that makes it possible to bring a future flow back to the present. It stands to reason that the reverse also exists, and it is called *accrual* (or *capitalisation*). Savings is one example of this. Individuals who pay their taxes once a year typically put money aside every month to pay off their tax. One option is to put their money in a passbook savings account, earning them interest every day because interest accrues daily.

We have a cash flow expected today, M_{today}, a cash flow expected in the future, M_{future}, and an applicable interest rate, r. The switch from one date to another is made as follows:

$$\text{Capitalisation: } M_{future} = M_{today} \times (1 + r)$$
$$\text{Discounting: } N_{today} = \frac{N_{future}}{1+r}$$

We will not go into how r is calculated because it is extremely complicated and depends on the identity of the parties involved. It should also be noted that each party can evaluate the transaction and obtain a different rate. While the credit risk is borne exclusively by the lender, the assessment of the cost or profitability of the transaction may be quite different on both sides (Airbus and the bank in the example above).

Capitalisation and discounting are fundamental parts of capital market finance. We will see some examples of how they are used later, but the basic idea is this: no risk analysis or valuation is possible without fixing a moment in time. This may be today or a later date, but for the sake of consistency, a single date must be established when studying a financial portfolio.

6. Why it matters

As we will often discover, the figures speak for themselves. At the end of 2016, the amount of debt outstanding in G20 economies stood at $148,997 billion:

($ billions)	2016
credit to the non-financial sector	**$148,997**
of which credit to the private non-financial sector	**$94,484**
of which households	*$36,598*
of which non-financial corporations	*$57,886*

of which credit to the government sector   **$54,513**

NB: In these statistics, "credit" includes: loans, negotiable debt securities and deposits.
Source: Bank for International Settlements Statistical Bulletin, December 2017.

These mind-boggling figures are steadily increasing and show how we are all living on credit. The characteristics of this debt are extremely varied, notably in maturity and collateralisation. But the fundamental elements remain the same: an interest rate that represents a credit risk, the price of inflation and the general availability of credit, driven by central banks.

The fact that financial institutions are not included in these totals should not come as a surprise and does not make things any less relevant. A bank is basically a creator of credit: its assets include the loans it has awarded and its liabilities include the debt it has taken on to get the liquidity it needs. What really matters is the debt that flows to the real economy, i.e. the debt that cannot be repaid immediately because it is tied up in non-financial production or consumption processes.

IV.   Valuation and Mark-to-Market

1.   What are we talking about?

Suppose you buy a share of the company XYZ for $100 today. You do not need to be a rocket scientist to calculate the value of your portfolio: $100. What happens if the price of XYZ changes tomorrow? If it rises to $110, you will be hugely tempted to cash in right away and increase your wealth by $10. On the other hand, if it goes down to $90, will you be honest enough to admit that you lost $10 or will you bury your head in the sand and convince yourself it is only temporary and the market will go back up? Of course, anything is possible; nothing is irreversible as long as you have not sold the share. The $10 gain or loss is therefore merely a potential – or latent – one, and will be realised only upon selling.

The discipline of reassessing a position daily using the market value as a benchmark is called mark-to-market (MTM). Despite its apparent simplicity, this is an extremely complex concept and the consequences of its application may surprise you.

2.   Non-financial considerations

As is often the case, the issues confronted on a trading floor can be found in other areas of life. The notion of MTM is widely present in industry, for example. Take the case of a car manufacturer. Its plants purchase raw materials, store them and consume them to produce vehicles that are then shipped to their owners. What happens when the prices of raw materials or spare parts change? Transparency requires the car manufacturer to reflect these changes in its accounts in one way or another. The accounts do indeed contain dedicated items for inventories; it is therefore normal that these values change with the reality of the market, i.e. actual prices.

Implicit in this approach is the fact that we expect an economic actor to have an explicit MTM policy for its activity. If an industrial company produces a good that becomes impossible to sell – for example, due to a manufacturing defect – we expect the loss to show in that company's accounts in order to reflect reality as closely as possible.

Unfortunately, this is easier said than done. How do we affect fluctuations in the value of inventories over time when purchase prices change so quickly? What about Total, the oil company, for example? The oil inventory is an important component of the business, so what should we do when it has been accumulated over a long period while prices have fluctuated considerably? One answer seems to make more sense than the others: an average purchase price should be measured and used to value the entire stock. In practice, this means doing and redoing an average for each barrel of oil added to the inventory.

Fine, but how should we recognise barrels exiting the inventory? What looks more like a barrel than another barrel? Do we have to mark them one by one to know the purchase price of the one we have just sold? To calculate a profit, you need to know both prices exactly and calculate their difference. It is easy to imagine how the situation becomes more complicated when we multiply the number of products, when inventory turnover increases, etc. Accounting theory has come to grips with these difficulties, and there are various methods to value inventories while intelligently taking entries and exits into account.

Here is a simplified balance sheet of an industrial company whose factories store raw materials:

Assets		Liabilities	
$100,000	Cash and cash equivalents	Debt	$200,000
$250,000	Stocks		
		Shareholders' equity	$150,000

The sheet is, of course, balanced.

Now suppose applicable accounting rules and a significant price change make it necessary to write stocks down to $200,000:

Assets		Liabilities	
$100,000	Cash and cash equivalents	Debt	$200,000
$200,000	Stocks		
		Shareholders' equity	*$100,000*

The balance sheet must remain balanced; otherwise the company is in default on paper. It does not matter which way you look at it: if the liabilities outweigh the assets, bankruptcy awaits.

The revaluation of stocks has an immediate impact on equity. It is a de facto loss to the detriment of shareholders. Several more issues then appear:

- The recognised result has tax consequences. The company has made a loss, which may be deducted from past or future earnings.
- By appearing on the balance sheet, the loss is realised for accounting and tax purposes, and yet inventory is not sold or liquidated, and the company may not even experience any particular difficulty. Its management is probably aware of price fluctuations in supply and has taken steps to get through this cycle smoothly.
- If the shareholders' equity is sufficient, nothing is lost. It is always possible to explain to investors that the value of their shares has declined, safe in the knowledge that the company's ordinary business could rectify everything. A balance sheet is merely a snapshot; it does not predict the future. But what would happen if shareholders' equity were low or insufficient? The loss would result in negative equity and therefore immediate bankruptcy. Does a revaluation of stocks alone justify putting the company into administration?

In terms of both tax implications and impact on equity, we need to ask ourselves when is the right time and what is the right benchmark for revaluing inventories. In other words, when should an MTM be applied and at which reference price, knowing that there may be severe consequences?

We will come back to this point a little later. What is true of inventories is also true of all other accounting items, whether assets or liabilities: an uncontrolled revaluation can quickly have serious implications. We have not really addressed the subject of price observability. In the case of an industrial company, it is easy to imagine that inventories and other physical assets are relatively simple to value. In the case of intangible or purely financial assets, the price may be difficult or even impossible to observe.

The accounting response to all these difficulties is the *purchase price* rule. All assets on a company's balance sheet must be carried at the prices at which they were acquired. Consequently, their price does not vary with market fluctuations. When assets are removed from the balance sheet – because the stock of raw materials has been transformed into finished products – the gain is recognised between the selling price and the sum of the average prices of intermediate products, which have not been revalued since their initial recognition[15].

OK, but this situation does not work either: what happens when a company's assets undergo an objective and considerable change in value? In the case of a bank for example, it holds all kinds of products, some of which are listed on exchanges and are widely traded, so using the acquisition value for these is objectively debatable. What happens when certain assets, such as derivatives, are contracts and thus inherently intangible?

3. Valuation and liquidity

Let us stop for a moment to think about liquidity. Everything we have talked about so far is based on the existence of a reference price, itself derived from real transactions. After all, what could be a better reference point than the last traded price? This presupposes that the asset being valued is fungible (interchangeable) with a mass of similar assets and that these are exchanged with sufficient regularity and transparency that everybody knows the characteristics of each transaction.

---

[15] This is obviously just the basic principle: although a balance sheet carries assets at acquisition cost in theory, there are many accounting and tax rules enabling these items to be revalued over time.

These are the fundamental conditions of an efficient and *liquid* market: a large number of transactions carried out under conditions of almost perfect transparency. Unfortunately, these conditions are not always met, and the best example for us to look at is real estate. The real estate market, even in a single neighbourhood, is far from homogeneous. It does not consist of fungible goods that are regularly traded on terms and at prices known to everyone. Estate agents are well aware of this, which is why they are still able to charge for their services in the internet age.

The structural illiquidity of real estate is a real difficulty when trying to value a property, however *standard* it may be. In some countries, transaction databases are not freely accessible[16], and even when they are, it is statistically possible to produce only average prices. Since each product is different from the next, using these averages is a tricky exercise biased according to whether you are buying or selling.

Valuation is not the most important concern, moreover. Sellers know full well that if they have to sell at the wrong time in the economic cycle, or if they have to sell quickly, they will be forced to accept a much lower price that cannot be estimated in advance. It is a vicious circle: the absence of transactions leads to price uncertainty, which in turn drives away sellers who will often prefer to wait for better visibility and stronger bargaining power.

Normally, this is when you expect the buyers to show up, but here is the thing: since most of them have to take out a loan, if the banks themselves are adopting a wait-and-see approach or are in trouble, there are no more buyers, whatever the price. This scenario is the textbook case of a real estate fire sale. A fall in the market scares lenders, and buyers are thin on the ground and those who remain lower their bids; meanwhile, sellers who are forced to liquidate their property then accept these significantly lower bids, which accentuates the precarious state of the market, and on it goes.

---

[16] This is the case in France, where transaction data are known to notaries and are not made public. Networks of estate agents have their own data that offer a certain visibility.

This example shows that illiquidity is the biggest barrier to a precise valuation[17], *let alone* a reliable and regular valuation, which MTM is by its very nature. The consequences for financial industry are apparent: the function of banks is to create money through credit, and real estate credit is therefore a very important component of the balance sheet of any retail bank. The illiquidity of the real estate market causes mirror illiquidity in banks' real estate receivables.

Take, for example, the balance sheet of a normal financial institution:

Assets		Liabilities	
$100,000	Cash and cash equivalents	Debt	$2,450,000
$2,500,000	Loans		
		Shareholders' equity	$150,000

It is an institution with a moderate leverage: balance sheet total of $2,600,000 and $150,000 of shareholders' equity, i.e. a leverage ratio of 5.77 % (= $150,000/$2,600,000).

Let us also assume that the mortgaged real estate which serves as collateral to the portfolio of loans has a total value of $2,600,000. This amount does not appear on the balance sheet because the bank would become owner of the assets only if the borrowers were to default.

You would not expect *all* borrowers to be able to repay their loans in full: an economy always has a default rate. What happens if the general economic situation deteriorates, prompting an increase in unpaid debt beyond what is generally observed? For example, if the outstanding amount is 5% and the bank has an orthodox MTM, it will have to write down its receivables, with a direct loss in equity:

---

[17] And therefore a major ingredient in all financial crises.

Assets		Liabilities	
$100,000	Cash and cash equivalents	Debt	$2,450,000
$2,375,000	Loans		
		Shareholders' equity	$25,000

Two things happen simultaneously:

- Shareholders' equity suffers immediately, and the higher the leverage, the faster the deterioration. In this situation, the bank will cease its lending activity almost instantly.
- It is hard to imagine an economic situation deteriorating to the point where many households are unable to meet their loan repayments without affecting the housing market as a whole. As regards MTM, the bank must therefore also revalue the portfolio of assets used as collateral. And this revaluation could easily result in a deficit: the bank carries $2,375,000 on its balance sheet for a portfolio which could be worth much less if the market is really bad.

The situation will undoubtedly develop into a downward spiral:

- To balance its books, the bank needs to seize and liquidate assets from defaulting borrowers so it can collect its receivables and restore its shareholders' equity. This will contribute to the price of the assets falling even more.
- Other financial institutions in the same geographic area will likely suffer the same negative effects on their receivables, with the same consequences: a forced sale of a certain number of assets seized as collateral.
- If prices continue to fall, banks will automatically see a decline in the collateral they hold, and therefore seek to accelerate liquidation.

These well-known mechanisms fully deploy over multi-year economic cycles. A downturn in the housing market also directly affects the morale of households, who glean that times are tough and see a decline in their net worth.

Hopefully, this provides a simple, concrete and extremely relevant example of how an MTM valuation affects the lending activity of a large financial institution. Beyond the understandable need to show faithful accounts, MTM has the potential to create a deadly spiral.

4.   Derivative products

Derivatives introduce two additional elements of complexity. By definition, these are intangible contracts, so no payments are recorded before expiry (see Chapter 7 "Cash and derivatives" for a detailed definition of a derivative). It is therefore impossible to show the contract on the balance sheet: a piece of paper that merely expresses a promise to pay or receive cannot appear in a company's assets or liabilities. Particularly since all derivatives have zero value at the outset of a transaction. Mathematically, this is brought about by something called no-arbitrage pricing, but intuitively the explanation is quite simple: no one would agree to enter into a contract knowing they will lose money. A derivative is doubly impossible to carry on the balance sheet: it is a contract, and its expected value (in the statistical sense) is zero. The other difficulty is that the value of a derivative depends on the value of its underlying. The easier it is to value the underlying, the easier it is to value the derivative (in general). And vice versa.

Here is a concrete example: suppose that corn is traded at $100 per tonne, and that the (theoretical) futures price at 3 months is $10 higher, which corresponds to the costs of storage, insurance, etc. (see Chapter 5 on deferred delivery for the definition of a futures contract). The buyer of a tonne of corn records a cash outflow of $100 and an inventory entry of $100 of corn on their balance sheet. By contrast, the buyer of a tonne of corn futures at $110 records nothing[18].

---

[18] What happens if they manage to buy it at $108 and not $110? Should they recognise a gain of $2, which corresponds to the difference between the "theoretical" value of $110 and the acquisition value of $108? This gain is real, but when should it be

If the price of corn climbs from $100 to $115 in the days that follow, the physical corn carrier and the futures buyer have potentially made $15 (the futures is now valued at $125, including the $10 from storage, insurance etc). It is quite logical to ask them to show this gain on their income statement and balance sheet by revaluing their inventory. This happens immediately for the physical holder but requires the futures buyer to record the product's MTM on their balance sheet.

This quick analysis has shown us that it makes no sense to recognise a derivative at acquisition cost. It can be valued only at its MTM, which must appear on the balance sheet since it generates a receivable or a payable – and *ultimately* a profit or loss.

5.   Mark-to-market and the financial industry

The various remarks we have made so far can be summarised as follows:

- To force an MTM approach on a financial institution is to subject it to economic cycles, with all that this might entail for its shareholders' equity and more generally its solvency. This characteristic is often called "procyclicality": the worse the economic situation, the worse the state of the banking system because its non-performing loans increase and its capital disappears very quickly. It is precisely in difficult times that the banking system must play a cushioning role by maintaining reasonably open access to credit for individuals and businesses alike.
- On the other hand, capital markets divisions within major international institutions, which use derivatives on a massive scale, must adopt an MTM approach for the simple reason that there is no other way to value their portfolio.

---

recognised? Today, based on a theoretical model, or in three months, when it is actually collected? In reality, it depends on a number of factors. Theoretical valuation of certain positions is possible, but tightly regulated.

The industry has resolved this apparent contradiction by splitting accounts into two:

- The *banking book* includes all positions for which a strict MTM is not required. These are often positions that are intended to be carried indefinitely, and for which an MTM process could cause procyclical effects that are difficult to control.

- The *trading book* comprises all positions available for purchase or sale, i.e. all assets, cash and derivatives whose purpose is to be turned over, i.e. bought and sold regularly as part of normal operations.

The Basel Committee has clearly defined the rules for including products in each of these groups, transferring from one book to another and the consequences of such transfers[19].

6. Mark-to-Model

However, there is an alternative to MTM for derivatives which are too complex or have an underlying that is too illiquid: mark-to-model. Some derivatives are so specific that they are only traded once. One example would be a client with a particular need, such as an insurance company wishing to hedge a hybrid exposure to interest rates and currencies, a large corporate seeking to take a risk on the joint evolution of the price of oil (or electricity) and the expected average temperature next winter, etc. There are plenty of others. The resulting derivative will not be listed: it is anything but standard. Moreover, its characteristics probably make it a complex product, for which there is essentially no market. It is difficult under these conditions to impose an MTM. The regulator therefore allows non-standard treatment.

A derivative is always the result of a price calculation model, fed by market parameters. If the price of the product cannot be observed directly, what about the parameters to which it is sensitive? In the examples above, interest

---

[19] See "Minimum capital requirements for market risk", Basel Committee on Banking Supervision, January 2016. Available on the Bank for International Settlements website (www.bis.org).

rates, currencies and oil or electricity prices can be observed and/or estimated. Anticipating the average temperatures over the coming winter is of course a tricky undertaking, but at the very least we can look back over the last 10 years. Once again, this idea of looking to the past to tell us about the future. It's still wrong, but what else can you do here?

The price calculated by the model will, by necessity, be considered the fair price. The use of this methodology is carefully regulated by the banking supervisory authorities and the internal risk control departments. It is easy to imagine how tempting it would be to prefer a favourable price that a model tells you is just right to an imposed, and potentially unfavourable, market price.

7. Why it matters

There are no figures here to justify the inclusion of this chapter in the list of fundamental concepts, rather a macroprudential approach. No one needs to be convinced of the need for, and merits of, a rigorous valuation of a financial asset or product. It's common sense.

But what is the relevant valuation? When should it be applied? When should it be imposed? Despite its apparent simplicity, this question does not have an immediate answer for all the reasons mentioned above. The financial industry is caught between two non-aligned constraints: constantly providing a true and fair view of its solvency – and to a lesser extent its profitability – and not being procyclical, i.e. fragile when the economic environment actually demands greater intervention. It needs to be strong enough to absorb losses, without compromising its ability to remain fully functional in a recession. It was this balancing act that dominated the Basel Committee's concerns and gave rise to long and technical negotiations.

V. Spot trading and deferred delivery

1. What are we talking about?

Derivatives (we will define this term precisely later) have been in existence for thousands of years. Historians have repeatedly discovered written evidence of transactions similar to our modern derivative contracts[20]. It is important to note, however, that in ancient and financially archaic societies, the underlyings of transactions were physical commodities: corn, oil, wheat, precious and non-precious metals, etc.

To explore the notion of spot trading and deferred delivery, we will look at the example of a wheat producer and a flour manufacturer. The producer has a simple availability problem: he has wheat to deliver only twice a year but is faced with a demand that is not seasonal. The solution is obvious: store part of the harvest and sell it one bucket at a time.

Producers, collectively and individually, have good reasons to adopt this sensible behaviour:

- If they sell only when they have wheat, the supply will be overwhelming after the harvest and extremely scarce at any other time. This situation, where supply dominates, leads to a large price variation between harvests (abundant supply, low price) and the rest of the year (scarce supply, high price).
- If only one or a small number of producers store the wheat, they will have a quasi-monopoly at non-harvest times and will be able to obtain a very good price.
- At the same time, while presumably being low, storage costs – space, insurance and security – are real. Each producer needs to think about this individually, even if generally they have an interest in moving in this direction.

---

[20] See for example: "Building the Global Market: A 4000 Year History of Derivatives", Edward Swan, Kluwer Law International, 2000, or "A Short History of Derivative Security Markets", Ernst Juerg Weber, 2008
(http://www.web.uwa.edu.au/__data/assets/pdf_file/0003/94260/08_10_Weber.pdf).

Interestingly, there is a solution to this problem whereby producers work together and agree that some of them will store wheat and others will not, with the former incurring a cost and therefore receiving additional remuneration. This might be an elegant solution, but it is illegal: it is the organisation of a cartel with all the consequences that has for competition. In this setup, wheat buyers would *almost certainly* not pay a "fair price", i.e. a price fixed by the fundamental mechanisms of fair competition.

Notwithstanding a cartel situation, one can easily imagine the supply and demand dynamics likely to take hold if storage occurs. It is in everyone's interest to spread out deliveries: the producers can enjoy a more even distribution of income, and the buyers are more confident that wheat will be available at a reasonable price away from harvest time. Another option is for the buyers, rather than the producers, to store the wheat. The effect, however, would be the same: wheat prices would be pushed down at the end of each harvest by reduced demand because the buyers still have stocks available.

In practice, a purchase of wheat takes the following form: the seller collects the agreed amount, the buyer takes delivery and everything is settled. An *immediate* transaction like this, with settlement and delivery, is a *cash* (or *spot*) transaction. But what if the buyer does not wish to take delivery immediately? He/she agrees to take delivery at a later date, for example in three months. Both parties can go a little further and agree on the price that will be charged in three months' time. This type of agreement is a contract concluded today, for a deferred delivery (in three months' time), at a price fixed today. This is a *deferred delivery* transaction, also called a *forward transaction*.

Several questions arise:
- Why enter into such a transaction? For the seller, because of the certainty of selling their stock or harvest later, i.e. to guarantee a future income. The buyer has exactly the same motivation: the certainty of finding wheat at a future date.
- Are the sale proceeds exchanged? No, there is no delivery and therefore no reason for the sale amount to be exchanged. If it were,

it would be a credit operation (the buyer lends money to the seller for three months), with all the risk that any credit operation entails: if the seller does not deliver the wheat, they must repay what they have received, which is possible only if they are solvent.

- What would happen if the price was not set today? This would not be a forward transaction, but a deferred spot transaction. If the two parties agree to exchange wheat in three months, at the price in effect at that time, they might as well wait three months and transact at that time. Neither of them has anything to gain by entering into a transaction today without setting the price: that would create a contractual obligation without any benefit since the final price of the transaction will be the same as it would have been if they had not met until three months from now.

- Finally, and this is the primary benefit of a forward transaction, everyone has guaranteed availability at a certain price known today. Not only does the producer secure an income, but the amount is fixed, whereas if they had just stored their wheat, the price would have been...what it would have been in three months. And the same applies to the buyer.

The forward contract is a *derivative* of the cash transaction. Basically, any cash transaction can be transformed into a forward derivative if delivery is deferred. Wheat is the *underlying* of the forward contract.

The forward contract offers certain advantages over a cash purchase, particularly in that it removes uncertainty about the future. But is it a panacea? Of course not. If I think the price of wheat will be higher in three months, is it in my interests to sell at a price set today? It is clear from this discussion that the forward contract is a powerful tool for regulating and organising the wheat market over time. But it does not offer the possibility of immediate speculation and raises the question of value: what is the three-month forward price of wheat compared with the spot price?

To do this calculation, one of the most fundamental in market finance, we will adopt an arbitrage approach and draw up a flow diagram. What are each party's cash flows and when are they received/disbursed? We know from Chapter 3 how to capitalise/discount flows, so if we bring all flows back to today we should be able to answer this question satisfactorily.

First of all, and this is fundamental in the world of derivatives, the forward transaction is a zero-sum game: each dollar paid by one party is received by the other. This symmetry makes it possible to focus on only one of the stakeholders. In this case, we will look at the producer. Arbitrage-based reasoning involves examining two theoretically different situations and establishing their equivalence: if we succeed, the economic flows will necessarily be equal, which will allow us to draw conclusions.

Situation 1: the producer sells their wheat (1 kg), at P_c (price per kilogram). The delivery is immediate, and they collect the amount of the sale.

Situation 2: the producer sells their wheat on a three-month forward basis at the price P_T. During these three months, they must store, insure and secure their wheat for a total cost of C (= carry cost, they must "carry" the wheat for three months. This price is reduced to an amount per kilogram for the sake of consistency). They therefore receive P_T - C on delivery.

Are these two situations comparable? In both cases, the producer has no more wheat (it has been delivered) and receives a sum of money. In the first case, however, they get the money right away, while in the other example they have to wait three months for it. To compare the two situations, we should pick a date and express everything on that date. Since the decision to trade forward or spot must be made now, the only reasonable choice is to bring all flows back to today. If the flow of situation 2 is discounted, the two situations are equivalent: the producer no longer has the wheat and has been paid for it.

So if we take r as the relevant interest rate between now and three months from now, we have:

$$P_C = \frac{P_T - C}{1 + r}$$

The calculation of r, which would assume knowing the risk associated with future flows and the identity of the stakeholders, is neglected here. However, since it is conceptually a perfect trade-off, r is theoretically very close to the risk-free rate. If we had capitalised the flows in three months' time, the result would have been the same.

This could also be expressed as:

$$P_T = P_C \times (1 + r) + C$$

The forward price of wheat is equal to the spot price P$_C$, plus financing r x P$_C$, plus the carry cost C.

What does this result mean?
- P$_T$ depends on P$_C$: the higher the price of wheat today, the higher its forward price. That makes sense.
- P$_T$ increases with r, i.e. a high interest rate increases the forward price of wheat, all other things being equal. This is also logical since a forward sale delays payment. The higher the interest rates, the more attractive it is to have money available immediately to invest it. In other words, the producer will want to be paid at least the opportunity cost of the money they cannot invest if they sell forward.
- P$_T$ increases with C, the carry cost. No surprises here: if it costs me to store wheat, I expect the person who generates this cost to assume it entirely; otherwise there is no reason not to sell spot at P$_C$.

This formula features (almost) all the basic elements of modern finance[21]. The same type of reasoning can be applied to various underlyings, particularly financial ones, and allows the exact price of a forward contract to be calculated, regardless of its characteristics. However, despite its simplicity, this reasoning does not explain all the subtleties of the situation. So now we will dig a little deeper and take a closer look, particularly at the risk inherent in a forward transaction.

2.   The 1855.com case

---

[21] Volatility is the one missing because it appears only in so-called *convex* products. See Chapter 14 on optionality.

Yours truly is one of 1855.com's unhappy customers. For those who do not know anything about this case, it is a classic Ponzi scheme applied to wine[22], i.e. a situation in which payments from new investors/purchasers of a product are used to remunerate old investors with a premium, which leads them to sing the product's praises, thereby arousing the growing interest of newcomers. The Ponzi pyramid mechanism is well known, so how does it tie in with a forward derivative? The business model of 1855.com was based on a logic of spot vs. forward trade-off, but sadly the logic was flawed. Let me explain.

Like any wine retailer, 1855.com offered mail-order wine for immediate delivery. Nothing new here: all they had to do was find a wholesaler and apply a big enough margin to cover advertising and marketing costs. However, 1855.com also offered *grand cru* wines *en primeur*, i.e. with deferred delivery – typically 2 or 3 years later. In practice, this meant the site collected the money, with a promise of delivery once the producer made the bottles available. Only the company did not actually place orders for the future deliveries in question. Doing so would have meant a forward contract with the wine producers for deferred delivery. Rather, the company's plan was to spot buy the bottles that arrived on the market at the time of delivery to the customer.

To repeat: if 1855.com had entered into a contract with the producers at the time of the customers' order, they would not have had any particular difficulty. But instead they gambled on forward vs. spot: buying a 2007 vintage in 2009, whereas the customer ordered a 2007 *primeur* in 2007. Wine prices have increased considerably and steadily over the last 15 years, and unfortunately this gamble proved disastrous: in 2009, the 2007 vintage could sell for much more than the 2007 *primeur* ordered in 2007. What is more, producers have *carte blanche* to distribute as they wish, and if they decide to reserve a vintage for a few select distributors, so be it. This quickly resulted in a catastrophic situation: to deliver the *primeurs* which had become overpriced, it was necessary to use money from current orders, and so the Ponzi pyramid went into action.

The lessons are clear:

[22] See for example "1855: the wine Ponzi scheme", *Les Echos*, 03/18/2013. (in French)

- The forward price is indeed calculated using the spot price, but it remains impossible to predict how the spot price will evolve in the future. Selling wine forward without having secured the inventory today is akin to speculating that the price will fall between today and delivery. Any form of speculation is a risky business.

- The example of wine introduces a new element. Could the 1855.com situation happen with wheat? Not really, because one bucket of wheat is the same as the next. The fungibility of wheat in space (between two producers) and in time (a current harvest and another in 2 years) would have solved 1855.com's problem: if they had managed to sell wheat forward 2 years before harvest, when the time came they could have turned to any producer to honour their commitment[23].

The complete fungibility (in time and space) of the underlying is therefore an important characteristic: if it exists, it is possible to deliver any good or service in the future. Now let's look at financial assets.

3.   Commodities and financial assets

Forward delivery has been in existence for virtually thousands of years on cereals and applies equally to other commodities: oil, natural gas, precious (gold, silver, platinum, etc.) and non-precious metals, but also much more exotic underlyings such as milk, soya, palm oil, sugar and cocoa[24]. How does all this apply to a financial asset such as a stock or bond? Let's revisit the two previous scenarios.

Situation 1: The holder of a share sells that share at its spot price. Delivery is immediate, and the shareholder collects the amount of the sale.

---

[23] There are, of course, different varieties of wheat. But the point still stands: the buyer would probably have accepted delivery of a variety similar to the one ordered, even if it meant requesting a price adjustment.
[24] See, for example, a breakdown of agricultural products on the Chicago Stock Exchange: http://www.cmegroup.com/trading/agricultural/

Situation 2: the shareholder finds a buyer who, for whatever reason, wants the share to be delivered in three months' time. Both parties agree today on the forward price, P_T. During those three months, two things happen: 1) the holder enjoys the benefits of ownership, namely receiving dividends d (or coupons if it is a bond); 2) the buyer does not have to pay the amount of the sale, so they accrue interest on this sum, at a rate r. To keep things simple, we will assume that r is a risk-free rate because the buyer does not want to run the risk of losing all or some of the amount they will soon have to pay.

As before, if we compare these two situations after discounting the flows to today, we find that they are identical, i.e. that their financial consequences are identical – the share has irrevocably changed hands at a certain price. Hence the following result:

$$P_C = \frac{P_T + d}{1 + r}$$

Alternatively:

$$P_T + d = P_C \times (1 + r)$$

The left side represents the situation of the seller who receives P_T at the end of the period and the dividends d over the period. The right side shows the situation of the buyer who has not disbursed P_C and receives interest $r \times P_C$.

So:

$$P_T = P_C \times (1 + r) - d$$

This formula is therefore the valuation of a derivative contract for the forward delivery of a financial asset. "The forward price is equal to the spot price plus financing minus dividends". This is the strict equivalent of the formula we saw earlier for wheat. The difference $P_T - P_C$ (or $P_C - P_T$ depending on the conventions used) is called the *basis*. "Basis trading" is the joint trading of a spot product and a forward contract on that underlying to try and capture favourable price differences between the *market price* and the *theoretical price* (as given by the formula above) of that forward.

1855.com was not only selling wine; it was engaged in basis trading, perhaps without even knowing it? Moreover, they did it on illiquid (no pun intended) and non-fungible assets, i.e. the perfect storm. As their bankruptcy shows, basis risk – which is a direct consequence of the joint existence of spot and forward products – should not be taken lightly.

4.   Solvency

It is time to introduce the issue of solvency. The spot buyer of a tonne of wheat leaves with his truck full. The forward buyer of a tonne of wheat leaves with nothing more than the word of the seller that delivery will be made when he shows up again 3 months later. This is significant but at the same time almost worthless.

First, a contract is only as strong as the legal system in which it was forged. The Anglo-Saxon system, for example, affords a central role to contractual law. As a result, not surprisingly, the United Kingdom and the United States have long been pioneers in financial innovation. British commercial power, founded on undisputed maritime domination for several centuries, was an important element in the development of liquid and prosperous capital markets in the 18th and 19th centuries because it created a demand. The actual delivery of the goods in question could take some time.

However, the law does not solve everything. It has, in particular, one major disadvantage: mobilising a mediator, and particularly a court, is a long and expensive process. For this reason, the financial industry has structured itself so it can provide a practical and effective solution: initial margins and margin calls (which we will cover further in Chapter 7 on derivatives). These mechanisms considerably reduce the risk of default whatever the characteristics of the participants, and have thus enabled trade to develop significantly.

5.   Why it matters

Analysing deferred delivery is particularly helpful because it sets the scene for all derivative products:

- It occurs frequently in real life, and there is a reason why it is chosen to introduce several abstract notions. When stocks, bonds and organised markets did not exist, humanity was already faced with the major problem of ensuring its subsistence in time and space, which presupposed the ability to trade efficiently. Deferred delivery is an extremely simple and powerful tool for solving very practical problems of this kind.

- Compared with a spot transaction, deferred delivery is a *contractual* arrangement between two parties with common (or indeed opposing, depending on how you look at it) interests. We will come back to this idea, but we can already state that all derivative products are built on the same principle, i.e. a contractual arrangement whose terms are discussed and agreed at the *outset.*

- There is always a mathematical relationship between the value of a derivative and its underlying. Although this relationship is straightforward here, we will see that this is not the case for options, for example. Reasoning by equivalence between two situations, i.e. an arbitrage-based reasoning, makes it possible to draw useful conclusions, if not establish a definitive valuation.

- The question of solvency arises immediately because, by design, the main transaction – the delivery of the goods in exchange for payment – does not take place until later.

VI.   Short-selling

1.   What are we talking about?

The idea that you can sell something you do not possess may seem strange, but that is exactly what short-selling is. Obviously, it does not mean you can auction off the Eiffel Tower to the highest bidder (even if there would be plenty of potential buyers); short-selling means entering into a transaction without being able to supply the buyer (regardless of whether the object of the sale is an intangible financial asset such as a security or real property such as a car).

Why would you want to sell something you do not have? To take advantage of a price drop and buy it back for less later. This is short-selling in a nutshell: getting favourable exposure to a price drop. We are all used to prices for everyday goods and services going up. And no matter how experienced they are, investors adhere to the old adage that the stock market "can only go up in the long term". Sadly, this is not always true; just look at the crisis of 2008. If that fails to convince you, take a look at the Nikkei's performance between 1980 and 2000. The same is said of real estate, either in physical or specialist corporate (REITs, or real estate investment trusts, for example) form.

The notion of inflation captures this idea, whether for conventional commodities or goods traded in far greater volumes or at far higher prices. Leaving aside the 2008 crisis, Japan is the only country in recent history to have experienced significant and sustained consumer price deflation. We can all relate to buying something to meet an immediate need or as a precaution, out of fear that it will cost more tomorrow. But, conversely, what should you do when you think that something is too expensive? Is it possible to make money from a transaction if the price of an asset that we "objectively" believe to be overvalued falls? Take real estate, for example. We have all felt that the prices in certain cities and regions are outrageous and must surely fall at some point. If your hunch turns out to be right, how can you make money on it?

Speculation is not the only motivation of a short-seller. Suppose you own and manage an inherited property portfolio. Since prices have soared, you are thinking about all those latent capital gains. The thing is, just a slight reversal on the market could see those gains decimated or wiped out completely. There is always the option to sell all or part of your portfolio to get your hands on those gains, but in doing so you obviously lose ownership of the real estate. If only there were a way to sell without permanently transferring ownership…

The "trick" is to obtain ownership of the asset temporarily, i.e. to *borrow it*, in order to be able to deliver it to the buyer. When the price has dropped (or even if it has not), the asset is bought back and returned to the person who lent it[25].

Take the example of the stock of a company called ToTo, whose price today is $100. For various reasons, you think that this price is not justified, and you wish to take out a stock market position that will make you a profit if ToTo's stock falls. It turns out that one of your friends completely disagrees and has ToTo shares in their portfolio.

The *modus operandi* is then as follows:
- You ask your friend to lend you the ToTo shares, i.e. to make them available to you, on the written proviso that you return the shares to them at a later date (not necessarily fixed today).
- You sell the shares on the market – and receive the proceeds of the sale, but we will come back to this point.

The sale itself is perfectly standard: you deliver the shares like any other seller. This is possible because you have borrowed them. The idea that selling short is "selling what you don't have" is actually slightly misleading: you end up delivering something you *do* have, but you just borrowed it temporarily.

---

[25] Short-selling is therefore very closely linked to securities lending/borrowing. Readers looking for a more technical analysis should consult the "Reference Guide to U.S. Repo and Securities Lending Markets" at the following address: https://www.newyorkfed.org/medialibrary/media/research/staff_reports/sr740.pdf

In the interest of full disclosure, there is another way to achieve a similar result: enter into a sale contract with deferred delivery. It is not necessary in this case to own the ToTo shares immediately, just to find a way to deliver them when the time comes. This can be done in two ways: borrowing them or buying them back. Intuitively, whichever method you choose, the gain or loss should be identical; otherwise risk-free opportunities arise and everyone would rush into them.

Some time later, you are proved right: ToTo is trading at $60 per share. Closing the position is easy: you buy ToTo at $60 and return the shares to their original owner pursuant to the loan contract that binds the two parties. You cannot argue with your profit: you received $100 from the initial sale, you spent $60 buying the shares back, so $40 goes straight into your pocket. The gain for your friend is less clear, but we will come back to that.

In principle, the borrowing transaction is easy to conceptualise. You can borrow a kilo of sugar from a neighbour, consume it and return a new packet one week later, so you can also borrow a security, use it (i.e. sell it) and then buy it back afterwards, no later than the contract expiry date.

If we take a closer look, however, questions arise:
- What is the lender's motivation? In the case of shares or a house, we are hardly talking about a kilo of sugar.
- What happens if the borrower of the security cannot return it?
- If the security has gone up or down, what happens to the lender? They lent their shares, but can they actually still sell the shares when they want? If so, how can they be sure they will keep all the profit (or loss if applicable)?
- Can you perform this type of operation on goods other than shares as soon as you are convinced that their price is too high?

2.   The lender's remuneration

If we assume that the situation of the security lender is not affected by the loan (and this assumption will be confirmed in due course), the transaction can be viewed like a rental. The borrower pays the equivalent of rent to do with the security as they please: keep it, sell it or maybe lend it to someone else. Interest rates are referred to as the "cost of money", and the same is true here: it is possible to lend and borrow financial assets just as easily as cash.

The amount of the rent depends on a number of parameters: the stock itself, the duration of the loan and the total size. It is fixed by a supply and demand mechanism. If a borrower is actively and urgently seeking an instrument, they will contact the market participants they assume have it in their portfolio. After doing the rounds on the market, they will choose the one who offers the cheapest rent, as any tenant would do. There is already a major issue here: for all this to work smoothly, there must be a large number of active market participants. And that means the stock cannot be rare: the more people who possess it, the less expensive it is to borrow. In practice, although we should be careful not to generalise, a few quantitative elements can be assumed here:

- Most borrowing or lending (B/L) transactions are short term, typically overnight. Unless explicitly instructed otherwise by one of the parties, the transaction rolls over from one day to the next at the same price by tacit renewal.
- Depending on the asset class (equities, bonds, etc.), rents range from 0.05% to 5% under normal conditions, sometimes much higher in exceptional circumstances. Pricing is a market mechanism. If everyone rushes in at the same time, the price will rise very quickly. And the opposite is true if the stock receives little attention[26].
- A B/L transaction requires a specific legal framework. Depending on the jurisdiction, the type of product and the choice of the parties, this framework may be a *repurchase agreement* or a *master securities lending agreement*. As we will see in the next chapter, B/L is therefore pure derivative.
- Legally, B/L is a transfer of ownership. This is a *temporary* transfer because the security must be returned at some point, but it is

---

[26] Certain situations, such as a takeover bid, can create a strong and immediate demand for a stock. The buyer is often short sold extensively on the back of speculation that the purchase will be successfully completed.

nonetheless an actual transfer of ownership. This is important for voting rights, dividends and so on.

- Because of the way it is constructed, a B/L transaction should never pass on to the borrower any of the benefits (or costs) that the lender would have been likely to receive (pay) if they had kept the security. In concrete terms, therefore, if a borrower receives a dividend on a security, they must pay it back in full to the lender. Similarly, if the borrower, as the beneficial owner, has the right to vote at a shareholders' meeting, they must respect the lender's instructions. All these elements are built into the contract, which is the backbone of the relationship.

The lender therefore has an immediate economic interest in lending their securities, particularly if they do not need them immediately. For example, an investment fund that owns securities and holds them for a long time may generate additional income by making them available to potential borrowers.

3.   Market risk

Suppose I borrow 1 $100 ToTo share today, at a rent of 1%. Immediately after receiving it, I sell it for $100. A month later, ToTo announces disappointing results, and the share price drops to $85. Very happy to have been proved right, I buy ToTo back at $85 and return the share to its original owner.

What happens on both sides of the B/L transaction? On my side, I received $100 when I sold the share a month ago. Then it cost me $85 to buy it back, so I pocket $15. This is my reward for having successfully speculated on ToTo's disappointing operating performance. However, I owe rent to my lender, which is calculated as follows:

$$R = \$100 \times 1\% \times (1/12) = \$0.0833$$

Thus 1% is the agreed rental price and 1/12 is the *pro rata temporis*: I owe only one month's "rent" because just like any tenant, I pay for the effective duration of use.

Now consider the lender. At the time of the transaction, they own the ToTo share; otherwise they would not have been able to lend it. When the company announces its results, they observe that the price drops by $15. The borrower (me) then contacts them and returns the share, accompanied by a payment of $0.0833, so they recover their asset but realise that it is now worth only $85.

Is this any different to what would have happened had they kept ToTo all this time? No: they lose $15 in both cases. But, by lending the share, they received additional income. What would have happened had they wanted to sell their share before the results were announced? They would have called me and exercised their right to recall the security at any time (unless explicitly agreed otherwise at the outset, the recall clause is always present by default). They would then have received it and been able to sell it, again, no different than if they had held onto the share to begin with. What would have happened if ToTo had paid a dividend during that month? I would have been obliged to pay it back in full to the lender[27].

This is the essence of a B/L transaction: it does not affect the economic situation of either party in any way, except for the rent which slightly enriches the original owner. The lender wins or loses depending on whether the stock goes up or down: precisely the same scenario as if they had kept it. Because they have borrowed, the borrower has no economic exposure. The security may or may not appreciate, but that is not the borrower's risk, just like it was not before the transaction. The trigger for economic exposure is the *sale*, not the borrowing transaction. This sale creates downside exposure: the short-seller earns money if the stock goes down.

4. Credit risk

So far so good, but why might the borrower not return the share when they are supposed to? It could be one of two things: either they are unable to

---

[27] This obligation is the default in all B/L contracts. Were it not, no one would ever lend their securities. In the real world, there is also an element of taxation. Dividends are taxed differently depending on the type and nationality of the holder.

return it because they simply do not have it – for example, they did not buy it back after selling it – or they are not in a position to meet their financial obligations, i.e. they are in default. Lending your car to someone you do not know clearly entails a certain risk that it will not be returned in the same condition, if at all. To deal with this situation, the borrower is asked to provide a guarantee, called *collateral*. In the case of a car rental company, the guarantee is insurance provided by a third party. It is impossible, however, to extend this principle to the capital markets because you would need bankruptcy insurance, which unfortunately does not exist (although some instruments get fairly close).

In the case of B/L, the collateral is essentially the full amount of the loan. This means that the transaction proceeds as follows: the lender delivers $100 of ToTo shares to the borrower, who in return pays $100 in cash. If by chance the borrower defaults, the lender immediately has the option (and legally the right) to use the $100 guarantee to buy back the security that will not be returned. If the share price has fallen, they will pay less than $100 and will therefore have to return the balance to the borrower. If the share price has risen, however, it will cost them more than $100 and they will register a loss. They are then entitled to ask the borrower for compensation for this loss since it materialised following a default. This is where things get awkward: if there is a default, we can assume that the defaulting party will not be able to pay off all their debts, and that a lengthy judicial, protection or liquidation process will be necessary to determine what can be reimbursed and to whom[28].

The case where the borrower is still solvent but does not possess the security when it is recalled is simpler. At the lender's request, they must comply, so they have no choice but to buy back or to borrow the missing security from someone else. The problem is not so much buying back the stock, but *having to* do so under duress and within a certain time frame.

---

[28] Creditors are repaid in order of seniority, with the government coming first. It should also be noted that the bankruptcy of a financial institution, as Lehman Brothers has shown, does not really lend itself to court protection. After all, in the absence of physical assets, a bank consists solely of intangible receivables and payables, so it is almost impossible to do anything other than liquidate the entire balance sheet.

So why might an investor wish to recall a portfolio security and sell it? Typically, a substantial increase in price, and this is the worst that can happen to a short-seller: the security was borrowed with downside speculation, so an increase in its price represents a loss. And if there has been an increase, it is precisely at this moment that the lender is most likely to recall their shares and sell them. Unless they want to be declared in default, the borrower has no way out and must return the shares. If they are unable to borrow them from someone else, they must buy them back, and at the worst possible time. That is why it is difficult to be in a short-seller position for any prolonged period of time: you are at the whim of both the market and the lender, who can recall their security at any time and will almost certainly do so at the worst possible moment.

5. In practice

In order to get a complete picture of how a B/L transaction works in practice, we still need to look at two things: margin calls and something called a "haircut".

We said earlier that paying collateral equal to the amount of the borrowed security reduces the borrower's risk of default. The problem is that if the value of the security changes from one day to the next, the initial collateral may no longer be sufficient. Two mechanisms are therefore in place to protect everyone's interests and accommodate the differences in value between the security and the collateral:

- the haircut is a safety margin for the amounts exchanged;
- the margin call is a daily payment to reset the position to zero.

In concrete terms, the different stages are as follows:

- I borrow 1 $100 ToTo share today with a haircut of 105 % (to make things easier, let's say there is no rent). I receive one ToTo share and transfer $105 (= $100 x 105%) to the lender.
- Tomorrow, ToTo is worth $110. The lender has only $105 to deal with a default on my part. This is not enough to cover their costs, i.e. the price they would have to pay to buy ToTo if I did not return their share. This amount is the market price, i.e. $110. The

counterparty will therefore initiate a margin call to redress the balance: the amount of collateral required is $115.5 (= $110 x 105 %) because the haircut must be applied in all cases. The margin call is therefore $10.5 (= $115.5 - $105), and it is up to me to pay.

- Two days later, ToTo is worth only $95. The lender should have $99.75 as collateral (= $95 x 105%), but they actually have $115.5. The margin call is now reversed, so they will pay me $15.75 (= $115.5 - $99.75).

- Eventually, I decide to close my position with ToTo still worth $95. I return the share, and my collateral is returned in full, i.e. $99.75. Supposing I never sold the stock, the flows on my side are as follows: - $105 - $15.5 + $15.75 + $99.75 = 0. I have not lost anything, nor have I gained anything, which is fair enough since the only effect of the transaction was to transfer the ownership of a ToTo share to me for a few days[29]. The lender's flows are the exact opposite of mine, so they haven't lost anything either.

This example again illustrates the mechanics of a B/L transaction: there is a transfer of ownership, but not of risk. Margin calls are used to ensure that the economic exposure remains with the original owner, regardless of the duration of the loan. This mechanism adds an important safety net: in the event of default, each party has an equal reserve, within the haircut (the security on one side, the collateral on the other).

6. What about real estate?

The above examples have all featured equities (and can therefore apply equally to bonds), but the question arises as to whether the same ideas can be applied elsewhere, to different financial assets or even tangible assets. Basically, we have just seen how it is possible to borrow a company's capital – debt or equity – to build downside exposure, i.e. sell it. Is it possible to speculate similarly on the decline of real estate? What about oil? Gold? Corn? Diamonds?

---

[29] Each flow gives rise to positive or negative financing from one day to the next, but we have ignored this to keep things simple.

A B/L activity requires a divisible underlying for which all partitions are fungible. Oil is one example: one barrel of oil looks exactly like the next. So I can borrow someone's barrels and sell them, while being reasonably confident that I will be able to replace them with identical barrels. The same goes for gold, corn, etc. Diamonds are a different kettle of fish: in theory, you can replace one diamond with another, but it is hard because you have to replicate its precise characteristics (color, size, clarity, inclusions).

Can you borrow a car and speculate that its price will decline? No, because a car wears out: if you borrow a car today with the intention of returning it a few days later, there is inbuilt depreciation even if you do not use it much or the model is specified precisely (colour, engine, options, etc.). The fact that new cars are constantly being produced with the same characteristics is not important: a company is likely to issue new shares every day, oil is extracted every day, etc. The quantity available for lending or borrowing potentially has an impact on the rent, but the principle remains.

Can you borrow a piece of real estate to sell it and buy it back afterwards? No: no two apartments are the same, even in the same building. Moreover, real estate is subject to wear and tear, so we have to draw the same conclusion: delivering an *identical* property is impossible. Being unable to sell a property short is one of the reasons why real estate is an asset class for which the idea of valuation is flimsy. Anyone who thinks prices are too high can sell only what they own. If they own nothing, all they can do is wait and hope for prices to fall. Price adjustments are therefore much slower than for asset classes where short-selling is possible, or even easy.

7.   Why it matters

The existence of short-selling has a profound impact on the inner workings of financial markets. Its very nature means that it creates the conditions for *symmetrical* price formation. It is extremely easy to speculate on the upside: just buy a security and wait. Moreover, you can often buy on credit, so you do not need to mobilize a vast amount of capital.

But what tools are available to participants who feel that valuations are too high and prices are likely to fall? Apart from short-selling, none. The existence of a market for lendable assets is therefore the assurance that the price of those assets is set by an exhaustive procedure that includes *all* agents, including and especially those with opposing views. The market is simply more efficient as a result. This is a subject on which there is plenty of research, particularly academic research, and it always leads to a similar conclusion.

Finally, as you will learn to your surprise in a later chapter, short-selling can be (slightly) diverted from its original purpose and serve as a means of (re)financing. It is one of the major tools of treasury management at major banks. Once again, the figures speak for themselves. The US dollar bond repo market tends to fluctuate between $2,200 and $2,500 *billion,* and the euro market is similar. So we are talking about four times France's GDP on these two currencies alone. In equities, the open B/L position is estimated at $890 billion globally[30]. Whichever way you look at it, these are extremely significant amounts.

---

[30] *Sources*: "Weekly Global Securities Finance Report", 23-30 January 2017, IHS Markit, "US Repo Market Fact Sheet 2016", SIFMA (www.sifma.org), "European Repo Market Survey June 2016", International Capital Market Association (www.icmagroup.org).

VII.   Cash and derivatives

1.   What are we talking about?

We have already encountered two derivatives in the form of a deferred delivery contract and a borrowing/loan transaction required to sell short. But we haven't yet defined exactly what a derivative is, and what it *is not*.

In trading jargon, a "cash" or "spot" product is a product whose acquisition is paid for in full. A cash transaction is said to "settle" when the delivery takes place. The process is (unsurprisingly) called *delivery versus payment*. Ownership changes immediately and permanently as a result. In order for this to happen, the buyer must pay the full price to be collected by the seller, unconditionally. A share, a bond, an apartment, a barrel of oil, or 1 kWh of electricity are cash products. A B/L transaction is *not* a cash product because: 1) the transfer of ownership is only temporary; and 2) the transaction is governed by a legally binding contract for a given period. It follows from this definition that the price of a cash instrument does not depend on the price of another product since it is known unconditionally at the time of transfer. In contrast, a *derivative is a contract whose value depends on the value of one or more other financial instruments called the underlying(s).*

A few points need to be clarified:
- The derivative is a *contract*. The purchase or sale does not generally give rise to any payment[31]. Both parties promise to abide by the terms of the contract, in the context of a *specific* transaction. In the case of a forward delivery, there will be an exchange of goods for cash on a date and at a price determined today. In the case of B/L, there is a transfer of ownership, payment of rent, right to recall at any time, etc.
- The simple terms buy and sell actually make no sense for a contract, but convention and practicality dictate that participants use these

---

[31] NB: the payment of an initial margin or a haircut has nothing to do with the contract itself; it is an *additional* security mechanism to ensure the solvency of the transaction. In other words, in an ideal world without bankruptcy, no initial margin or margin call would be necessary.

labels. Since there are generally only two parties to a derivative contract, the term buyer is adopted by the one who realises a gain if the price of the underlying has risen on expiry. The other party is the seller.

- Like any contract, the derivative has a maturity date on which it ceases to be effective. There is usually a final flow exchanged by the parties or delivery of a cash product, and the contract is extinguished. This is a huge difference compared with the underlying itself: a share or bond does not expire, and an inventory of corn can deteriorate, but this is predictable and has nothing to do with a date on a document agreed by two participants. The maturity of a derivative is also called its expiry date.

- A contract carries an inherent financial risk that one party will not behave as it should because it is unwilling, or more likely unable, to do so (typically as a result of bankruptcy). In the event that one of the parties does not want to fulfil its obligations, it is always possible to go to court and cite the contract which stipulates the rights and obligations of each party. This is particularly relevant when the level of technicality is asymmetric. Since the 2008 crisis, many legal proceedings have been initiated in France, the United States and other countries against banks that had supposedly sold their customers (e.g. municipal authorities) incomprehensible products leading to disaster when the markets did not evolve as expected. Asymmetry of information and understanding is a major challenge, and regulators around the world have legislated massively to ensure that the responsibility for producing information and explaining risks lies with the most competent and educated party, i.e. the bank that manufactures the products. These situations rarely occur between two professional counterparts because there is no such asymmetry.

- Since the derivative transaction does not generate a payment at inception, there can be significant risk. Take the case of a deferred delivery. For producers, selling forward is not a problem: they can often organise their production and storage to deliver on time. But what if a speculator enters into a forward sale contract with the intention of buying corn a little later to then deliver it? If the price of corn rises significantly, the speculator will face a potential loss, and a big one at that. Although no payment is requested at the conclusion of the sale, they could be exposed to massive amounts. This is because derivatives enable a potentially devastating leverage effect. So the industry has structured itself to control that risk (see below).

- The contract can keep everyone happy. In other words, it is for the parties to define what they want - at least in over-the-counter (OTC) products (see Chapter 10 on OTC and listed products).

- A derivative contract is a "zero-sum game". On expiry, if one party records a loss, the other party must record an equal and opposite gain. This is completely different from many other instruments: a corn producer who sells their crop should logically see a gain, as should the buyer who is likely to use that corn to make their own products. The seller of a stock may make a profit or loss depending on how much they paid when constructing their portfolio, but the buyer's situation has no effect on this. The essence of a derivative is to transfer risk, which takes the form of a cash flow at maturity known as the payoff.

- The final flow is always known precisely on the expiry date. Although the prices of many instruments are totally random and unpredictable in today's world, they are observable at all times. Forecasting is impossible, but observation is not. On the expiry date, the payoff of a derivative is known and observable. The difficulty comes in pricing it *between* inception and expiry.

To understand the power of a derivative, let's go back to our wheat producer. In the case of a cash sale, they must have the wheat available, packaged and ready for delivery. Otherwise, they can negotiate a convenient deferred delivery date(s) with the buyer. Although the producer will not receive the proceeds of the sale immediately, it is a way to secure future income. Forward selling is future planning.

2. Leverage

Let's return for a moment to the leverage in the wheat example we used in the previous section, putting ourselves in the buyer's shoes. In a cash transaction, the buyer must pay the full amount immediately and take delivery, with all that entails in terms of transport, storage and insurance. If they accept a forward contract, there is no immediate payment to make nor any material contingency to consider. The benefits of this situation are fairly obvious. If you are convinced that the price of wheat will rise, you can buy tonnes of wheat forward and sell them on sometime later, without mobilising any capital. The problem is that if things do not unfold as planned, the risk of bankruptcy is extremely high for speculators with a small capital base.

This is not an imaginary threat. The leverage of a derivative is potentially enormous. To prevent too much damage, counterparties usually impose a cushion at the outset of each transaction. This cushion, known as the initial margin, is proportional to the nominal amount traded and restricts leverage[32]. For example, a speculator wishing to buy $10 million of wheat could be forced to deposit $1 million with the counterparty, giving them maximum leverage of x10 if they had only $10 million in cash. If they were allowed to deposit only $100,000, leverage would be x100, meaning that for every $1 of movement in the price of wheat, they would gain or lose $100.

3. Credit risk mitigation

In practice, the initial margin is not enough to fully mitigate credit risk, i.e. the risk that a counterparty will not be able to meet its obligations when the contract expires. Suppose, for example, that I want to go long on ToTo, whose shares are now trading at $100. With $100,000 in my pocket, I decide to buy 10,000 ToTo shares for a nominal fee of $1 million. I enter into a contract with a counterparty who agrees to deliver the shares one month from now.

A month later, the stock is trading at $110. I have to honour my contract by paying $1 million to receive 10,000 shares. Of course, I do not have the full amount, so I have to liquidate my position for $1.1 million in cash. Assuming

---

[32] This is exactly the same as the haircut in a securities lending transaction; the name differs depending on the type of derivative.

everything runs smoothly, my net gain is $100,000, or 100% of the capital I had at the outset. That's the beauty of leverage.

But what happens if ToTo is worth only $80 in a month's time? The proceeds of the sale will be just $800,000, which is not enough to cover the $1 million I have to pay. Considering my initial capital of $100,000, I am $100,000 short and in default.

There is nothing hypothetical about this situation, even for large financial institutions. We have already discussed the tool that allows us to address this problem, or at least to mitigate it: margin calls. In practice, when two participants are negotiating a derivative, logic dictates that the contract should include an initial margin to restrict leverage and a margin call mechanism, typically daily, to help build or rebuild a safety cushion.

The transaction therefore takes place as follows:
- I find a counterparty willing to sell me 10,000 ToTo shares forward in a month's time. The contract is signed with an initial margin of 10% and margin calls, so I make a payment of $100,000 to the seller.
- The next day, ToTo is worth $95. I have potentially lost $50,000 (= $5 x 10,000 shares), even if this loss has not yet been realised. For its security, the counterparty will ask me for a payment of $50,000 to restore its initial margin. If I am unable to make this payment, the counterparty will have the right to immediately close the position and use the initial $100,000 deposit to pay itself back. If this deposit is not sufficient, they would have full discretion to take legal action and seek reparation. So I have paid $150,000 so far. If I do not have that amount handy, I cannot maintain my position.
- If the next day the stock rises to $107, the margin call of $120,000 (=($107 - $95) x $10,000 shares) is in my favour, so I receive that amount. If I decide to sell ToTo, the gain of $70,000 (sale at $107, purchase at $100) is mine.

And so on until the contract matures. A daily statement of cash flows shows that, however the security evolves, the eventual gain or loss is calculated as the final price (at maturity of the contract) minus the initial price (on inception of the contract). But the presence of margin calls is key to limiting the risk that a participant would be likely to take and therefore ensuring that everyone remains solvent.

4. The problem of valuation

The valuation of a financial product means assigning it a price. We looked at the pros and cons of this practice in Chapter 4 "Mark-to-Market". In the case of a derivative, there are two types of valuation:

- Pricing at *expiry* allows the final flow to be calculated on the basis of the established contract (the payoff). This flow depends only on the value of the underlying(s).
- Pricing *before expiry* is more complex. Some derivatives are not tradable, i.e. once they have been created they can no longer be exchanged. In most cases, however, a derivative can change hands in the same way a contract can be transferred. So we need to know how to value it. Nowadays, the regulator also requires that the holder of a derivative be able to make an independent valuation. An additional reason for wanting a daily price, if we needed one, is being able to perform risk analysis, i.e. an analysis of how sensitive this price is to different parameters.

The valuation of a payoff before maturity depends on the derivative in question, but in most cases it is no trivial matter. Chapter 14 on optionality sheds light on the specific case of options, which no one knew how to value – rigorously, at least – before 1973 and the Black-Scholes formula. Since then, many different methods have been developed, tested and sometimes adopted.

One of these, the Monte Carlo simulation, is extremely popular. It is based on the following idea: if S is the price of an underlying (i.e. in practice a random variable), we can *simulate* the path taken by S between today and when the derivative matures. As we saw in the chapter on market prices, a lognormal distribution is often used to model a share price. For each of the paths, we get a value of S at expiry, S_T. And for each S_T, we get a value of the derivative. By taking the average of these, we get an estimate of the price of the derivative today.

The logic of this method may seem strange, but it is quite similar to the one we encountered several times when looking at statistical expectation. By taking a very large number of different paths on S up to date T, and considering that it is easy to get the value of the contract on expiry if I know S_T, I can calculate what I would be willing to pay today, *on average*, to benefit from the payoff of the contract.

Monte Carlo methods are invaluable because they are conceptually simple, but they do have two weaknesses:

- The first is well established: to simulate the path from S to S_T, we need to make an assumption about the behaviour of S, for example that its behaviour is lognormal[33]. This is nothing more than wishful thinking.

- The second is the nature of the method. The more paths are simulated, the more accurate the estimate is because a larger area of what is possible is covered. Computing power and speed are therefore important. The precision of the estimate – i.e., the uncertainty about the price obtained – varies, as does the inverse of the square root of the number of simulations ($1/\sqrt{n}$). This means that to get an estimate which is 10 times more accurate, you need 100 times more paths, which, in turn, requires significant computing power.

5. Physical delivery and cash settlement

I have indicated several times that calculating the payoff of a derivative when it matures is simple. But how does it work in practice?

At maturity, the contract is executed: a value of the underlying is used as a reference and the contractual clauses are strictly applied. Take, for example, the case of a deferred delivery. You bought 1 tonne of wheat at $100 for delivery in 3 months. At the time of delivery, the reference price of wheat is

---

[33] A slight generalisation on my part. This applies strictly to equities only. Other assumptions are made for interest rates, currencies, etc.

set at $110, so it is at this price that the contract expires and that you must buy the wheat. Hang on, didn't we say that the deferred-delivery price was fixed today and not at maturity? Absolutely, and we can use margin calls to reconcile the two:

- You buy wheat forward at $100 today.
- Over the next three months, spot wheat increases from $100 to $110, so that is the price used for expiry of the deferred delivery: three months from now, you buy the wheat for $110.
- Between now and three months from now, the derivative contract (deferred delivery) is subject to margin calls in your favour from $100 to $110, so you will have received $10 by the time the wheat is due to be purchased at $110, which brings the net price back to $100 as agreed. As we said before, the margin call mechanism ensures that only the last available price is significant. Without margin calls, the deferred delivery must be made at $100 and you would need to remember the price at which each contract was initially concluded[34].

The delivery of wheat is obviously a physical delivery, and this is quite common in the world of commodities, particularly oil. There is another way to end a derivative, called *cash settlement*. In this case, no physical exchange takes place. The contract is executed when one counterparty pays a sum of money to the other. In the case of the above deferred delivery, the final margin call between the price on the day before expiry and the reference price on the day of expiry constitutes the cash settlement. If the contract was entered into at $100, the sum of all margin calls is $10, which you receive over the period. The contract does not stipulate that you receive delivery of wheat, so you must buy it spot on expiry. It is worth $110, so taking into account the margin calls, you do indeed pay out $100. The result for you is the same except that, in one case (physical delivery) you do not have to make a final purchase, while in the other case a spot purchase is necessary. But the price of that purchase does not matter because the initial price is guaranteed by the margin calls.

---

[34] Margin calls therefore offer more than a credit risk mitigation service.

The reference price of the underlying used to calculate the final value of the derivative has several different names, including Exchange Delivery Settlement Price (EDSP) in Europe and Special Quotation (SQ) in Asia. It is mutually agreed by the counterparties or set by the exchange when the transaction takes place on an organised market.

6. Is it really that simple?

Well, no. I have chosen some examples that are fairly easy to follow. There are endless scenarios for the payoff of a derivative. There may be an optional component, several underlyings, different asset classes (equities, interest rates, currencies), etc. There are even derivatives of derivatives. Financial engineers have boundless imaginations. Of course, there is the question of the valuation and risk of these products. But as we have seen, financial engineering provides us with a fairly simple generic method to calculate the price of virtually any derivative: the Monte Carlo simulation.

Except that this price is wrong because the original assumption (lognormality) is wrong. Faced with this inescapable truth, the industry for a long time settled for an approximation: at first glance, the reasoning would appear to be correct, so the price is acceptable[35]. OK, but the losses start to accumulate if there is a financial crisis: because of the way they are designed, all simulations underestimate extreme risks. A more recent alternative approach is to go back to the drawing board to refine the models without making assumptions about lognormal prices. But no one knows the *actual* distribution of those prices, making this apparently more rigorous approach much more difficult to follow.

---

[35] The industry calls this "model risk" as opposed to a market, operational or human risk.

7. Why it matters

This is important for two fundamental reasons.

First, derivatives are a powerful innovation in how all kinds of risks are managed and spread in the international financial system. Even with all those valuation problems, they allow an open redistribution according to the appetite and constraints of each agent. The cost of risk, whatever it may be, is therefore assessed extremely accurately. Risk itself becomes "divisible": everyone can make an informed choice as to what to take, keep or hedge. This is real and significant progress.

Second, the figures once again speak for themselves. Open positions in derivatives of all kinds are colossal:

Global open OTC derivative positions	2015
Foreign exchange contracts	$70,446
Interest rate contracts	$384,025
Equities and indices	$7,141
	$461,612

Global market capitalisation	2015
Americas	$27,943
Asia	$23,141
Europe	$15,876
	$66,960

Marketable debt securities	H2 2016
	$21,655

NB: All figures are in billions of US dollars.
Sources: Bank for International Settlements, periodic statistics (www.bis.org) and World Federation of Exchanges, 2015 statistics (www.world-exchanges.org).

The capitalisation of all global stock exchanges is approximately $67,000 billion, while that of bond markets is $21,655 billion.

Derivatives are worth five times more than the amount of outstanding shares and bonds. Interest rate contracts are the largest pool, accounting for 83% of the total.

Speculation – through leverage – is of course one of the reasons that derivatives have been so prominent in the global financial system. But they do have other uses.

VIII.   Risk measurement and management

1.   What are we talking about?

Risk is present in various situations in all walks of life. As you might expect, a risk arises when there is a possibility that *something does not go as planned*. OK, but whether you are in a trading room or anywhere else, you cannot predict the future. The concept of risk management is therefore to encapsulate uncertainty within an intelligible *analytical* framework.

An intelligible analytical framework is an environment that attempts to quantify uncertainty and allows action to be taken accordingly. In concrete terms, in the case of a financial portfolio, it means answering the following question: how will the portfolio behave if the market moves one way or another? How much will it gain or lose in such scenarios?

These questions cover two different and complementary lines of thought. The first is sensitivity analysis: to which parameter is my portfolio sensitive? Do I really want to carry that sensitivity? How can I hedge this risk and at what price? The second, more general, approach is scenario analysis, which seeks to quantify an average or maximum potential loss based on hoped for or feared circumstances.

In both cases, the general idea is one of *differential* reasoning. Knowing the composition of the portfolio today, as well as the current values of the parameters required to value it, how does its valuation change when a risk factor evolves or, particularly, when all the factors evolve at the same time in a scenario made as realistic as possible?

It is important to note that risk analysis and valuation are distinct, even though all the modelling for valuation is a prerequisite. A valuation seeks to determine the most accurate or probable value of each instrument. This value is widely obtained using a mark-to-market methodology, and sometimes mark-to-model. Implicit in this idea is the notion of *liquidation*: the fair value of an instrument, by definition, is the one at which I can liquidate my position. In risk analysis, it is not the instantaneous value that matters, even less so the value that allows the position to be unwound, but the change in this value when there is a change in one of the parameters or the price of one of the underlyings.

The preferred tool for risk analysis is therefore differentiation, a useful mathematical tool to study the *variation* of a function. Let's take a closer look.

2.   Partial derivative

Suppose you have a derivative D in your portfolio, the value of which depends on the price of its underlying P, wheat for example. Not surprisingly, the price of the derivative contract also depends on interest rates r, storage costs s, time T to maturity, and perhaps some other parameters:

$$D = D(\dots, P, r, T, s, \dots)$$

What happens if P increases *slightly*, say by an amount h? For example, if P is worth \$100 per tonne, h can be arbitrarily set at \$0.10. The exact value does not matter because we just want to see how D behaves for P of around \$100. If D$_{\$100}$ is the price of D when P = \$100, what you would like to know is the price D$_{\$100+h}$ when P increases by h. And what would really be useful is an idea of the difference D$_{\$100+h}$ - D$_{\$100}$, i.e. the change in the price of the derivative due to the change in the price of the underlying. In mathematics, this exercise is called derivation[36] or differentiation:

$$f(x_0 + h) - f(x_0) = h \times f'(x_0)$$

where f'(x_0) is the derivative of f in x_0. This assumes that f(.) is derivable, but if it is not, it is still possible to calculate the quantity d defined by:

$$d = \frac{f(x_0 + h) - f(x_0)}{h}$$

[36] Do not confuse the derivative product, whose value depends on that of its underlying, and the derivative of a function that addresses the issue of its variation. The two totally different concepts are juxtaposed here.

that looks like the derivative. For our purpose, let's assume that it is always possible to obtain a usable derivative or to calculate it in approximate form as above[37].

Applied to our problem, we get the result:

$$D(\$100 + h) - D(\$100) = h \times D'(\$100)$$

This equation reads as follows: if the price of the underlying increases by h, the price of the derivative increases by h x the derivative of D. To know the variation of D, it is therefore sufficient to know its derivative.

Here's an example. Suppose at $100, D'($100) = 0.75. For every dollar change in the price of wheat (h = $1), the value of the derivative contract will increase by $0.75 (= $1 x 0.75). Conversely, if D'($100) = - 1.5, a $1 *increase* in P will lead to a $1.5 *decrease* of the derivative. In the most general case, without specifying the nature of the contract D, it is impossible to know whether its derivative is positive, negative, greater than 1 or smaller than -1.

As we will see in Chapter 15 on delta management, D'(P$_0$) is called the product delta and is a fundamental quantity. But what about the other elements that contribute to the formation of D? It is easy to extend our logic and calculate derivatives with respect to each of them. The notation must then be extended to the notion of partial derivative:

$$D(P_0 + h) - D(P_0) = h \times \frac{\partial D}{\partial P}(P_0)$$
$$D(r_0 + h) - D(r_0) = h \times \frac{\partial D}{\partial r}(r_0)$$
$$D(s_0 + h) - D(s_0) = h \times \frac{\partial D}{\partial s}(s_0)$$

where $\partial D/\partial V$(P$_0$) is the derivative of D specifically on the variable V, at point P$_0$.

---

[37] With a few exceptions, for example a binary option with a value of 0 or 1, the derivatives we use have a derivable price. A numerical simulation is sometimes necessary, but a calculation like the one for d described above produces results that we can use.

Concerning time, it is more common – and more telling – to look at tomorrow's value, i.e. with one day fewer until maturity. This indicator has a name, the theta Θ:

$$\Theta = D(T-1) - D(T)$$

This is exactly how much the portfolio will have earned or lost between now and tomorrow, *all other things being equal.* Even if all other things are never equal in real life, the idea is that this is the variation in value due to the passage of time alone.

All these indicators are called the "Greeks" of the position, and essentially they convey sensitivity to each of the risk factors. The first step in a risk analysis is therefore to calculate them exhaustively for all risk factors. The regulator requires these figures to be produced *at least* once a day. In practice, they are often calculated in real time. The huge merit of this approach is that it produces a set of homogeneous numbers that can be compared in time and space. From one day to the next, and from one trader to another, it thus becomes possible to monitor the instantaneous risk in the vicinity of the market at a time t. Not all Greeks are important to all activities. An index options trader will not have the same needs as his interest rate or oil counterpart. Nevertheless, the partial derivative approach can be extended to any type of trading.

Because of this, the risk limits on a trading floor are essentially imposed on the Greeks of each operator's portfolio. Whether on delta (dependence on the underlying), theta (dependence on time), vega (dependence on volatility) or rho (dependence on interest rates), traders receive strict limits that are scrupulously monitored by their control departments. A trader bound by limits tailored to their activity can therefore operate correctly within the framework of their mandate, not beyond. While necessary, rigorous Greeks surveillance is not sufficient for truly effective risk control. It is still, however, the first port of call[38].

---

[38] In the Jérôme Kerviel case, for example, the position was wrong. Kerviel inputted fictitious transactions to reduce the apparent risk in his portfolio. Clearly, monitoring Greeks would not have magically flagged a problem here. A simultaneous cash flow analysis would have detected the size of the real hidden positions.

If the sensitivities have been calculated and are within allocated limits, is there any more you can do? Can you sleep safe in the knowledge you have a satisfactory and exhaustive picture of risk? Not yet: the second part of risk analysis is to evaluate average or maximum losses in an unfavourable scenario.

3.   Scenario analysis

While it is useful to know that a given instrument could potentially lose $0.5 for each dollar of decline in the price of wheat, an estimated total expected loss if the price of wheat fell by 10% tomorrow is even more instructive. To get there, we need to simulate the valuation of the entire portfolio. If it contains a derivative contract on 10 tonnes of wheat, and wheat is worth $100 a tonne, a loss of 10% results in a drop of $10, i.e. a capital loss of $50 (= $10 x 0.5 x 10) on 10 tonnes. This figure immediately resonates: "at -10%, I lose $50". No room for doubt there.

A scenario-based risk analysis therefore aims to calculate losses based on the current sensitivities of the portfolio and using reasonably sound market variation assumptions. This second point is crucial. For example, if we look at a downward market shock of, say, 10%, how should we apply that decline? Is it 10% on an index like the S&P 500? If so, should we assume that each of its components falls uniformly by 10%? Hardly: each stock is unique, so how they react to bad news – a terrorist attack, a new president being elected on an uncertain or even worrying platform, a country voting to leave the European Union, all of which have happened recently – differ considerably. This means that we still have to use assumptions, for example: "I apply a 10% drop to the S&P 500 as an index, but the fall in each constituent stock is calculated based on its specific correlation to the market. The same applies to securities that are not in the S&P 500".

It's back again, that fundamental problem of finance that keeps rearing its ugly head: using the past to predict the future. Certain institutions – sometimes at the regulator's behest – use real scenarios: the Russian crisis of 1998, the bursting of the dotcom bubble in 2000, the bankruptcy of Lehman Brothers in 2008. Using real data has a certain virtue because that is how things actually unfolded. On the other hand, it assumes that the past will replicate itself exactly, which is more wishful thinking. And what about underlyings that either did not exist during these previous crises or have since disappeared? In any case, the overarching problem remains: chance cannot be easily modelled, and the distribution of market prices is leptokurtic. This is a devastating perfect storm for risk controllers the world over. When it comes to things going wrong, reality will always be scarier than fiction, and as we saw in 1929, 1987 and 2008, this unfortunately happens regularly[39].

In any case, even an erroneous risk analysis is an analysis of sorts and provides an indication of the scale of the potential losses. In fact, this is their primary *raison d'être*: regulators demand that these analyses be produced, regardless of their theoretical validity, to obtain a measure of financial stability. How much is an institution exposed to an unfavourable scenario and does this drain its capital to such a degree as to threaten its solvency? Of course, management is interested in this measure, but a particular form of scenario-based analysis is imposed for regulatory reasons: the value at risk (VaR) and its dark-days cousin the stressed VaR.

4. Value at risk (VaR)

VaR is a measurement that has existed formally since the 1920s, albeit not with the same name. The key question a market participant often asks is: what is my estimated maximum loss? The same question has also occupied national and international regulatory authorities for almost 100 years: if VaR is an acceptable way of measuring risk, even catastrophic risk, should we not impose a minimum amount of equity capital in proportion to VaR on all participants? After all, it would be another way to establish a concrete, relevant and fairly unarguable capital requirement to protect everyone, individually and collectively, from a participant's default.

---

[39] We are not even talking here about the fact that sensitivity analysis itself has limitations. As this is a derivative analysis, i.e. approximate, it is no longer acceptable for violent and significant movements.

VaR really came to the fore when the president of one of the largest American investment banks, Sir Dennis Weatherstone of JP Morgan, asked for exactly that: a simple report containing the bank's maximum loss every day. That was in 1989. Today, regulators widely recognise the method and impose capital requirements accordingly.

There are several types of VaR, and whole books are devoted to it, so no need to linger here. If you are interested in learning more, there is plenty of material out there. We should, however, reiterate the basic point: in the absence of precise knowledge of the distribution of returns on financial assets – whatever they may be – any risk calculation will be based on numerical simulations and/or historical scenarios, and as we know, this produces false results. We can't say it enough: the idea of looking at the past to gauge the future is deeply rooted in the collective conscious.

5.   Hedging a risk

A risk is said to be *hedged* when it has been neutralised or mitigated. On a trading floor, a multitude of products are sensitive to a multitude of risks. The key is to reduce at least some of them to low and/or acceptable levels.

This is the other great use of the Greeks mentioned earlier. The first is to quantify, and therefore to enable control. The second is to enable a choice of which risk to incur or eliminate. Consider a portfolio P in which there is a risk r – for example interest rate, currency or underlying risk. The risk of P is measured by its sensitivity to r. In addition, we have an instrument I, which we know to be extremely sensitive to r[40]. We can construct a portfolio H, being P plus certain quantity q of I: H = P + q x I

Consequently, by deriving and considering that the sensitivities are linear, i.e. they add up:

$$H'(r) = P'(r) + q \times I'(r)$$

---

[40] For example, an interest rate swap for an interest rate risk, or a foreign exchange transaction for a foreign currency exposure. In practice, the product I should be as "pure" as possible on risk r; otherwise hedging r may bring about other types of risk.

If q is chosen so that:

$$q = -\frac{P'(r)}{I'(r)}$$

then H'(r) = 0, which is also written as:

$$H(r + h) - H(r) = h \times H'(r) = 0$$

The value of H is independent of h, and therefore unchanged if r increases or decreases slightly. The factor r disappears from the portfolio and H is *hedged against r*. Chapter 15 on delta hedging explores this procedure in more detail, but it is clear that if there is a suitable instrument I(r), it becomes possible to hedge any portfolio against r.

This is also one of the reasons why derivatives have multiplied so rapidly in the last 20 years. The post-Black-Scholes realisation that an extraordinary number of products can be modelled (relatively) simply led us to discover that an extraordinary number of risks can be hedged.

Depending on their mandate, traders may therefore choose to incur one risk or another, provided their limits allow them to do so. For example, an equity trader will usually have low interest rate or credit limits. Conversely, a fixed-income trader will have no permission for equity exposure.

However, not everything can or should be hedged:
- Not surprisingly, a risk-free position earns you nothing. So hedging everything should not be a goal in and of itself.
- Some risks may disappear only to resurface concentrated in the hands of a limited number of institutions that are forced to incur them. One of these is inflation: there are inflation derivatives that transfer the risk to the only participant that can actually manage it, the state, through the issuance of inflation-linked bonds. Conversely, some products (such as weather derivatives) allow a risk that no one really knows how to assess to be redistributed. It is sensible and worthwhile for a utility company to hedge against the risk of low temperatures in winter which would lead to an increase

in demand with which it cannot cope, but this implies that someone agrees to take out the opposite position.

- Not everything can be hedged: the risk of terrorism and the risk of a particular electoral outcome are impossible to hedge using derivatives because they are one-off or rare events. It is obviously possible to insure oneself – that is, to buy an option whose value represents the replacement cost of a house, or the price of a human life if such a thing can be calculated – but insurance is not strictly speaking a negotiable instrument.

6.   Operational risk

We have focused all of the above on the notion of market risk, i.e. the intrinsic randomness of market prices when they result from an efficient formation mechanism. These are not the only risks out there: the nuclear accidents at Three Mile Island, Chernobyl and Fukushima are edifying proof of this. It took an unlikely accumulation of anomalies in the day-to-day operations of these nuclear plants for a serious nuclear incident to occur.

But you don't need to go nuclear, as it were, to prove that operational risk exists and should never be neglected. Take the case of US financial services firm Knight Capital. It was 1 August 2012 – a morning like any other. Within 20 minutes, Knight Capital lost $440 million, a loss that exceeded its equity capital and available cash flow. It was virtually instant bankruptcy for a business that had been healthy just a few minutes earlier[41]. The following weekend, Goldman Sachs bought Knight Capital to prevent a liquidation and benefit from a technology that had been considered very efficient up to that point.

So what happened? During a typical test session, a very large quantity of orders – we are talking about hundreds of thousands – was sent into the real market, in *production*, instead of being sent to test servers. It was an IT bug, or rather a series of bugs, since the orders were routed to the wrong

---

[41] More informed readers may wish to see the analysis by Nanex, a company specialising in high-frequency data: http://www.nanex.net/aqck2/3522.html.

destination and the hundreds of thousands of executions received were not identified by the system. Nobody became aware of the catastrophic failure until it was too late[42].

An IT problem is a textbook example of operational risk. Whether there is a power outage, a network component blowout or an established bug, modern finance relies so much on its information systems that even temporary downtime can have dramatic consequences.

Just like with nuclear risk, you would have to be pretty smart to predict the series of unfortunate events that would result in disaster. International regulators have long been aware of these circumstances and have responded with the main tool at their disposal: capital adequacy. The reasoning is always the same: there is no point in trying to predict the future; the safest thing is to ensure that participants can survive a crisis and this is achieved by increasing the necessary capital cushion. Today, the cushion dedicated to operational risks is calculated as a proportion of earnings from the last three years.

Finally, it should be noted that, in the specific case of high-frequency trading, institutions wishing to maintain trading algorithms are required to report them to exchanges and to ensure strict governance so that the source code of the algorithms is audited by developers other than those who wrote it and undergoes a cycle of precise and documented tests.

7.   Liquidity risk

So, have we covered everything now? Not yet. The collapse of Lehman Brothers and the shockwaves that followed on the international money markets showed how fragile these markets are when a first-tier institution fails. The results were immediate: since nobody was able to predict or prevent the risk of default, the only appropriate stance was to not take *any* risk. In particular, the US money market froze almost immediately in the

---

[42] The orders were intended to test the system load. For a security quoted at $99/$100, the algorithm sent orders to sell at $99 and buy at $100 for 100 securities each time. Each purchase/sale therefore resulted in a $1 loss.

days following the collapse of Lehman, and it became almost impossible for major banks to refinance themselves beyond the very short term, i.e. a few days.

This situation led the Basel Committee – which is responsible for producing the masterplans for international regulation – to examine the question of liquidity: can an institution whose assets have an average maturity of two years, for example, reasonably finance itself on a day-to-day basis without running a significant risk if it finds itself unable to borrow? And even if the problem is not its own situation? This is what Lehman revealed: all the US banks suddenly found it extremely difficult to finance themselves, even though they were not *directly* engulfed in the bankruptcy.

Monitoring and managing liquidity[43] risk, i.e. the ratio between assets and liabilities contracted to finance them, was therefore a cornerstone of the Basel III regulatory framework. Two measurements have emerged: the liquidity coverage ratio (LCR) and the net stable funding ratio (NSFR). To keep things as simple as possible, let's just say that the purpose of the LCR is to allow a bank to continue to operate normally for 30 days. Its calculation includes inflows and outflows over a 30-day period and requires the creation of a liquidity reserve sufficient for the bank to survive if it could no longer find financing over that period. The NSFR is similar but over a period of 1 year, with significant methodological differences. The LCR came into force in January 2015. The deadline for complying with an NSFR of 100% or more is scheduled for 2018 but has not yet been finalised.

Could the adoption of these prudential measures have saved Lehman? It's hard to say, but the answer is probably yes. There are now so many regulatory requirements that all the aggravating elements would have been addressed: market and credit risk, balance sheet structure, capital adequacy, excessive dependency on short-term financing, etc. Everything would have been oriented towards greater sustainability, although obviously at the expense of much lower profits.

---

[43] Liquidity here is taken in the monetary sense, i.e. literally the ability of a bank to finance its assets with its liabilities. Not to be confused with the liquidity we have already encountered which described the ability to buy or sell any asset easily, regardless of size.

8.   Why it matters

Some chapters of this book end with a presentation of figures, others with a reminder or highlighting of the fundamental concepts. The conclusion of this chapter is rather more straightforward: why should we care about all kinds of risks in the financial system? Because not caring *continuously* is simply a recipe for disaster. A trading floor is inherently risky, and catastrophe is never far away if the stars don't happen to align for anyone who falls short of a vigilance bordering on paranoia.

The "financialisation" of the economy at the end of the 1990s, regardless of whether you think it was a good thing, created a symbiotic link between the banking industry and the real economy. The latter no longer functions without ample funding organised by the former. This is nothing new, but it has placed a growing number of demands on the economy, starting with financing consumption, which is the main driver of growth in all modern economies, developed or otherwise. Again, we may rue it, but consumers around the world can no longer live without credit. At the same time, savings rates are high in many countries. The financial industry is a stakeholder in all this: it creates credit, it organises the circulation of risks, it participates in the global allocation of financial resources (and therefore savings), and so on.

The problems are therefore as follows:
- everyone knows that market prices are deeply random;
- mathematically simple models are false, and those that make more allowance for extremes are complex to manipulate;
- *it is absolutely* necessary to have a risk analysis methodology that is correct at the very least and as exhaustive as possible;
- history shows that all the really severe economic and financial crises have rendered all the simulations obsolete.

What are we supposed to do? An initial response is provided in this chapter. By normalising sensitivity and scenario-based analysis, we can get an idea of maximum losses. The regulator then adds a multitude of safety cushions to cope with extremes. The immediate consequence is to severely reduce the financial industry's profitability and seriously impair its ability to act as an intermediary. Only time will tell how this will all play out.

IX.   Collateralisation

1.   What are we talking about?

We have already come across two examples of collateralisation: borrowing/lending a security to sell short and, more generally, putting up the guarantee needed to ensure the smooth execution of a contract, i.e. a derivative. Collateralisation involves backing a receivable with a series of financial flows which aim to ensure that the receivable is *executed* when it becomes due. Just like a derivative, this receivable may vary over time. Of course, if it remains constant, it is much easier to collateralise[44]. This is not a question of ensuring the solvency of one of the parties; we are concerned here only with one receivable at a time[45] .

For a long time, large financial institutions have been obliged to systematically collateralise their transactions with each other and with organised markets. End clients – investment funds, corporates, insurers – on the other hand, have not always been subjected to these constraints for quite understandable reasons. Setting up a guarantee mechanism with regular adjustments creates potentially significant management costs[46]. In addition, when dealing with well-established companies with a low-risk industrial base, many banks were willing to forgo explicit guarantees.

---

[44] I have chosen a financial definition here. In a property loan, the collateral is a physical asset rather than a series of flows.

[45] Typically, receivables on fixed-income products or securities loans are not necessarily fungible. It all depends on the legal framework of each of the contracts and the jurisdiction in which they were concluded. Identical derivatives pertaining to separate legal entities, even within a corporate group, are not receivables that can *automatically* be aggregated.

[46] There are two types of these costs: direct, whereby human resources are needed to manage the flows and associated risks; indirect, whereby collateral immobilises cash, which is often somewhat or extremely rare in the non-financial industry.

The bankruptcy of Lehman Brothers forced a reassessment of these practices. The European Market Infrastructure Regulation (EMIR), for example, imposes strict collateral requirements on derivatives, depending on the product and counterparty. In practice, this means that an international financial institution will not be bound by the same obligations as an industrial group for which the use of derivatives is secondary to its main business.

2. In practice

In the world of derivatives, collateralisation is based on two types of flows: the initial margin (IM) and the margin call (MC).

The initial margin is the safety cushion established at the beginning of the trade and is generally defined as a percentage thereof. For the most common derivatives, it is between 5% and 10% of the nominal value, depending on the type of product and the volatility of the underlying – which captures the variability of the product and therefore its risk. For example, in the case of a $100,000 wheat futures contract, the initial margin will typically be $10,000. Who pays it? The least solvent of the two counterparties, i.e. in practice the smallest or simplest[47], or neither if the regulator deems that they qualify for exemption. There are also perfectly normal situations in which no collateral is taken, namely when one of the parties is a central bank. Understandably, no one worries about the long-term solvency of an entity that prints money. The same does not apply to a country because countries have been known to default.

In the case of securities lending, there is an actual change in ownership so the amount is at least 100% plus a "haircut", depending on the underlying. The haircut is the additional value applied to an asset to obtain the collateral value. For government bonds, it is generally 2-5%, and for equities 5-10%. In concrete terms, this means that someone who lends a security – and therefore

---

[47] As we will see in the next chapter, in the case of a product listed on an organised market, everyone must pay the initial margin, regardless of the size or type of participant. This is the price to pay to benefit from the explicit guarantee of the market.

loses physical ownership – can expect to receive collateral of between 102% and 115% of the value of that security.

In all cases, the initial margin is returned when the receivable has been paid or has disappeared because either the product has expired or the position has been unwound. Typically, if the buyer of a wheat forward contract sells it on, they recover their 10%. Similarly, if the borrower of a security returns it, they recover their 105% if that is the amount they paid as an initial margin.

What happens if the receivable changes in value? The margin call resets the transaction, i.e. restores an initial margin as if the transaction had been entered into on that day.

To illustrate the operation in detail, and to answer some additional questions that will no doubt arise, let's consider the example of an investor who wishes to buy 1 share of the ToTo company with deferred delivery a month from now:

- Today, the investor needs to find a willing counterparty (typically a trader in a bank). They succeed and are offered an initial margin of 15%. If ToTo is trading at $100, they will have to pay $15. This is the only flow: the actual stipulation of the forward contract does not give rise to any payment.
- The next day, the price of ToTo climbs to $107. To protect itself from investor default, the bank wants to have a 15% cushion at all times, i.e. $16.05 (= 15% x $107). This is the role of the initial margin: it must be present *continuously* to protect the execution of the contract. On the other hand, because the share price has increased, the investor stands to gain $7 if they hold the share directly and sell it. In these circumstances, if the investor were to default, the bank would take possession of the ToTo share and benefit from that gain of $7, which in fact belongs to the investor. Collateralisation is intended to secure a receivable, not to transfer profits unduly. The bank will therefore pay a margin call of $5.95 (= $7 - ($16.05 - $15)) to the investor. The ($16.05 - $15) represents the increase in the initial margin that it can claim, and $7 the gain that it would realise if the investor were to default, a gain that must be returned because

it does not belong to the bank. Everything happens as if the investor had cashed in their gain in advance.

- A day later and ToTo is trading at $80. The initial margin is $12. But the investor's potential loss is $27 (= $107 - $80). Why take $107 as the reference price when the contract was bought at $100? Because the day before, the investor cashed in the gain from $100 to $107. This gain was $5.95 (= $7 minus the initial margin adjustment). They must therefore pay today the potential loss compared with yesterday. This makes sense: if they can cash in a gain in advance, they should have to pay for a loss. The investor must therefore pay $22.95 (= $27 - ($16.05 - $12)). The ($16.05 - $12) represents the amount of initial margin that they recover.
- The next day, fed up with all the toing and froing, the investor decides to unwind their position at $95. As it no longer has an open position, the bank cannot collect an initial margin, so it returns all that it has received, i.e. $12 (amount from the previous day, see above). And it owes the investor the change in value between the previous day and today, i.e. $15 (= $95 - $80).

It is fairly easy in this example to see that the investor lost $5, which corresponds exactly to the difference between the purchase price of $100 and the sale price of $95:

Sum of flows (from the investor's perspective) = - $15 + $5.95 - $22.95 + $12 + $15 = -$5

The IM + MC mechanism introduces nothing extraordinary from the investor's – nor the bank's – point of view, except that on each day they had to cash in their gains and cover potential losses. So there are daily cash flows, which give rise to financing (ignored in the example above), but in the end everything happens as if the initial margin and margin calls had never existed[48].

---

[48] If ToTo had paid a dividend, the bank would have had to pay it back in full to the investor. If a deferred delivery contract contained no such clause, nobody would ever trade any. All in all, the effect of a delayed delivery for the investor was to create a

This example makes it very clear that there can be no collateralisation without a regular valuation – daily, in practice – of the contract. It is for this reason that the EMIR texts impose constraints on how and how often valuation takes place. This logic – considering that the investor can default every day – obliges the bank to collect losses but also to disburse gains. As mentioned before, the systematic mark-to-market valuation mechanism means we can concern ourselves only with the current value of an investment.

3. Other forms of collateral

There are variations to the scenario I have set out above. In particular, I assumed that all flows were exchanged in cash. This is not always the case because it is possible to transfer an asset instead of cash.

For example, in the above case, the investor could pledge their house as collateral to the bank, assuming it is accepted. The bank would then find itself in the situation of having to sell the house if something went wrong, which is not necessarily its primary area of expertise, and for that reason it is unlikely to accept. Logically enough, the only type of collateral the bank would accept is an asset that it could liquidate quickly and without affecting its price. In practice, this means another share, a bond or a foreign-currency amount.

The idea of collateralisation *in kind* to avoid immobilising capital in cash is attractive. But what is the fair remuneration of this collateral? If an investor has a choice between different asset classes, which one should they deposit with third parties? For large financial institutions with complex balance sheets, this is a particularly important issue. For example, the European Central Bank regularly publishes a list of all the assets that it accepts as

---

leverage of $100/$15 = 6.67 times. Who lent the investor the unpaid $85? The bank, which will therefore take a cut as payment for its services.

collateral for its refinancing operations: sovereign bonds, quasi-sovereign bonds, but also securitisation issues, i.e. repackaging of bank loans[49].

4.   Why it matters

Remember the Bank for International Settlements (BIS) figures on outstanding derivatives (Chapter 7)? $461,612 billion. The BIS gives another statistic on these positions, the "gross market value", i.e. the "mark-to-market": this is the loss or gain that is unrealised because the contracts have not yet expired.

(USD, billions)

OTC derivatives	Gross market value *(end of 2015)*
Currencies, foreign exchange	$2,579
Interest rates	$10,148
Equities, indices	$495
	$13,222

Source: BIS, periodic report on OTC derivatives, www.bis.org

It is this amount of $13,222 billion that is (hopefully) collateralised and whose credit risk is therefore greatly reduced. For the record, the GDP of the United States was $18,861 billion at the end of 2016, and that of France $2,181 billion. As is often the case, the figures speak for themselves.

---

[49] By issuing a bond, a government finances itself without collateral. Not so for a central bank, whose role is not to finance the economy or any expenditure, but to conduct monetary policy, i.e. to steer interest rates and the money supply. A central bank therefore never lends without collateral.

X. Over-the-counter and listed products

1. What are we talking about?

In all the examples so far, a derivative product was traded by two identified counterparties with opposing interests, for example a wheat producer and a manufacturer of processed food. These are known as over-the-counter (OTC) transactions; their terms depend on the respective needs and negotiating power of each party.

Significant elements for determining the price include the proven or estimated solvency of each party, the size of the transaction, the various guarantees that can be provided, etc. The identity of the buyer or seller could also have an impact: buying wheat futures from a speculator who does not have any stock does not necessarily result in the same negotiation as buying from a seller who is an established producer with abundant stocks and the experience of maintaining them.

Without wishing to oversimplify things, it is easy to imagine how a market left to bilateral negotiation alone can quickly crystallize around a small number of players who have earned the right to participate thanks to their size, longevity or influence, or a combination of these factors. This state of affairs is certainly not conducive to liquid and efficient exchanges, i.e. in which the laws of supply and demand operate freely to form an economically significant equilibrium price – which is the market economy's Holy Grail. Moreover, continually renewing negotiations is unnecessarily time-consuming.

Given derivatives' degree of innovation, the industry has gradually structured itself to encourage the emergence of a market that is as liquid and efficient as possible by addressing the following problems (among others)[50]:

---

[50] As in many wholesale markets, established participants do not necessarily set out to be transparent. However, the most critical obstacle that *everyone* wants to remove is that of solvency: how can you ensure that everyone honours their debt? Since no one can accurately assess the creditworthiness of any economic agent, the problem of credit risk must be addressed *collectively*, not just for small players.

- enable as many players as possible to participate, whatever their type, size or solvency;
- structure the market to avoid the formation of explicit or implicit cartels that could manipulate prices in their favour[51];
- standardise products and more generally procedures to eliminate all unnecessary negotiation as a prerequisite to a transaction;
- structure a guarantee mechanism to ensure that all participants honour their obligations;
- ensure uniform and binding risk management for all participants;
- disseminate the maximum amount of information as quickly as possible – including trade prices – to enable the most efficient allocation of resources[52] in the economy.

These elements are not mutually inclusive, but reinforce each other. An effective guarantee mechanism enables a larger number of participants by allowing smaller players. An obligation of transparency makes collusion (more) difficult because everyone is bound by the published prices. A large number of players also allows more efficient price formation, higher volume and *de facto* less volatility.

The solutions to these circumstances differ widely according to the underlying instruments, countries, regulatory authorities and available technologies. Sometimes only certain aspects are covered. But in all cases, the solution lies in establishing a centralised, regulated and open market, whose rules are imposed on and known to everybody, i.e. a securities exchange. The exchange then assumes two fundamental responsibilities: price formation and *post-trade*, i.e. counterparty risk management.

---

[51] The problem of manipulation organised by an oligarchy is a recurring and major one; it is intrinsically difficult to eliminate, even for an electronic exchange open to all, because it just takes a different form depending on the circumstances.

[52] Very concretely, for example, spot and forward prices participate in the calibration of long-term investments in the oil industry. If they were not widely disseminated, very few agents would be able to plan their investments efficiently. Only those in possession of that information could plan ahead, giving them a competitive advantage.

2. Price formation

In essence, an organised market must allow supply and demand to meet without constraint to establish a rational equilibrium price, whatever the good or service traded. In order to fulfil this requirement, most organised markets have adopted the following principles:

- Access is open, albeit through authorised intermediaries;
- Trading is anonymous;
- Transaction data is public[53] and disseminated as quickly as possible, i.e. in real time;
- All participants are on the same footing, i.e. no operator is entitled to preferential treatment. This is essential, for example, in relation to pricing. A stock exchange may offer a sliding price structure as volumes increase, but this must be offered to everyone. Similarly, if it offers miscellaneous services – e.g. setting up a network, colocation in its data centre – the price must be the same for everyone. This has serious consequences: unlike any commercial company, a stock exchange cannot segment its clients and has limited flexibility on its pricing policy.
- The stock exchange maintains an *order book* on each product open for listing. This book contains the buying and selling interests, i.e. the prices and quantities available on both sides. These are firm orders: once transmitted and recorded, they are likely to be executed immediately unless they are cancelled.

When trading on a product is administered by an exchange, the product is said to be "listed" there. An (actual) order book of a share on Euronext is shown below by way of example:

47.555	2,574	7
47.550	2,525	8
47.545	2,216	7
47.540	3,263	7
47.535	3,069	7
47.530	3,080	9
47.525	1,441	6

---

[53] For a fee, of course. The same is true for historical data: available for all, but often for a fee.

		Price	Shares	Orders
		47.520	1,831	7
		47.515	1,745	7
		47.510	294	3
2	232	47.500		
7	1,133	47.495		
3	618	47.490		
4	781	47.485		
6	1,421	47.480		
5	1,195	47.475		
5	1,025	47.470		
2	539	47.465		
2	539	47.460		
2	739	47.455		

In pale blue (top table) you will find the sell orders, in pale red (bottom table) the buy orders. Each line aggregates all orders received: there are 7 sellers at $47.555 for a total of 2,574 shares. Similarly, there are 7 buyers at $47.495 for a total of 1,133 shares. The *first limits* are $47.50 and $47.51, i.e. the highest purchase bid and the lowest sell offer. The difference between the two, $0.01 in this case, is called the spread. Note that the spread here is higher than the "tick", i.e. the minimum price variation, which is $0.005[54].

As you can see, there is no indication of the identity of the participant in this table. Even after execution, anonymity is (more often than not) maintained at the clearing house level (see post-trade below). There is no limit on the number of orders a participant may place, amend or cancel.

An order book provides crucial information on the *liquidity* of an instrument: it allows investors to know the price at which they can carry out a transaction, *at that moment*. For example, a buyer of 100 shares knows that it will be possible to buy them at $47.51, unless the order book has changed between the order being placed and being recorded by the stock exchange. Similarly, a buyer of 500 shares knows that they can buy 294 at $47.51, but will have to pay $47.515 for the balance. And vice versa for a seller, of course. If an aggressive buyer *increases the offer* to $47.51 for 978 shares, the order book shifts:

---

[54] As an aside, share prices are not continuous, but discrete. Even if the tick is low — $0.005 in this case for a price of $47.5, i.e. 0.01% — it is not zero.

		47.525	1,441	6
		47.520	1,831	7
		47.515	1,745	7
6	684	47.510		
2	232	47.500		
7	1,133	47.495		

The new first limit of $47.51 substantiates the portion of the 978 shares that could not be bought at $47.51: 978 - 294 = 684. Logically, there is only one order at that limit. This information is then disseminated by the exchange and participants can adjust their interests accordingly.

Of course, the liquidity in the order book is only the visible part, the fraction that participants were willing to show. It is very possible that a buyer will want to acquire far more shares than the number visible on the stock exchange. Should they display their entire order in the book? Yes and no: if they do, this information will be widely disseminated, inducing potential sellers to come forward. This is why exchange prices must be public. On the other hand, if, for example, the buyer wishes to purchase 50,000 shares and displays them (say at $47.51), it is almost certain that nearby offers ($47.515, $47.52...) will be gobbled up, pre-empted by speculators with the following reasoning: if the buyer really wants to build up their position, they will end up paying more and it will be possible to make a profit on securities sold to them. This balance between displayed and addressable liquidity is crucial to how paper and electronic order books work.

Exchanges apply a strict price and time priority rule to ensure fair access for all participants. They give priority to purchase orders with the highest price, and to those recorded in the system earliest where the price is the same. For example, if purchase order #1 arrives at $47.515 and purchase order #2 at $47.52, the second will be executed first even if the offer is $47.515 like in the order book above. The size of each of these orders does not matter. Once purchase #2 is served, purchase #1 will be executed in turn. In the case where two purchase orders are received at $47.515, the first to be received will be executed first, and if there is still offer volume at $47.515, this volume will be given to the second order[55].

It quickly becomes apparent that the priority mechanism is the cornerstone of an efficient market[56]. For example, anonymity is not strictly necessary, even if it probably helps avoid some of the problems of yesteryear, like when order books still relied on an auction house, i.e. physical interaction between traders. Similarly, restricting direct access to the exchange to a limited number of members does not change anything except facilitate the general organisation and allow better risk monitoring. Each member in turn can open accounts for clients, including individuals, and assumes its share of responsibility to ensure that each client has financial standing and expertise that are commensurate with the risks they want to take.

Historically, most stock exchanges were mutualised institutions, i.e. their capital was held by members. This ensured independence from political and economic authorities and an alignment of the exchange's interests with those of market participants. Exchanges that charge for their services are keen to encourage transactions since fees are generally proportional to volumes[57]. It is also in the interest of members to have access to abundant liquidity. Moreover, a typical stock exchange was generally endowed with the right to regulate its members, under the supervision of a higher authority. This vision of self-administered regulation is deeply rooted in the United States for example, the idea being to let the industry structure itself freely, while maintaining an administrative supervision of last resort.

---

[55] This is a continuous open market trading cycle. In reality, the exchange opens and closes every day (at 9 am and 5:30 pm for Paris). Opening and closing are special moments governed by auction mechanisms during which only price priority persists – all orders received before the auction are identically eligible and rank equally. If there is not enough quantity to serve everyone at the opening price, buyers and sellers are served on a pro rata basis according to the size of the orders they have transmitted.
[56] There are alternatives to the price and time priority rule, such as priority to price and size, whereby all orders at the same price are served in proportion to their respective size.
[57] Exchanges often used to be non-profit associations. Strictly speaking, their mandate was therefore to create conditions for a fair and orderly market while merely covering their costs.

The main weakness of this setup is that it evolves according to the interests of those who benefit from the status quo, i.e. typically the largest and best-established players. Or more precisely, it does not evolve *outside* those interests. In the United States, for example, which has the longest tradition in this approach, stock exchanges have experienced difficult periods linked to actual or supposed dominant positions. In the early 1990s, the NASDAQ was sued by a large number of investors after two academic researchers uncovered order book behaviour for which they could offer no other explanation than the collusion of the participants[58]. It was also during this decade that the first electronic communication networks (ECNs) appeared, providing the same services as existing exchanges but with more efficient technology and at a much lower cost.

The wave of deregulation in the late 1990s brought about sweeping changes in market structure, first in the United States and later in Europe. The exchanges gradually demutualised and listed their own shares to enable more active governance, make way for genuine innovation and finance acquisitions. After all, what better way of dealing with a bothersome rival than to buy them out? Around the time of the millennium, major moves started to happen. Dominant exchanges sought to buy smaller competitors or engage in mergers of equals when an outright purchase was not possible. Many of these mergers were blocked by antitrust authorities. Euronext, for example, the exchange that lists – among others – French, Dutch, Portuguese and Belgian shares, and itself the result of a number of mergers, was denied a marriage with Deutsche Börse in 2015 on the grounds that the combination would have created a monopoly on derivatives trading. Even more recently, the merger of the London Stock Exchange and Deutsche Börse was blocked by the European Commission because it would have resulted in a monopoly on bonds[59]. This was the third time the two exchanges had tried to merge. Mergers have been attempted all over the place, with varying degrees of

---

[58] See "Why do NASDAQ Market Makers Avoid Odd-Eighth Quotes", *Journal of Finance*, Vol. 49, No. 5 (December 1994), William G. Christie & Paul H. Schultz, followed by "Why did NASDAQ Market Makers Stop Avoiding Odd-Eighth Quotes?", *Journal of Finance*, Vol. 49, No. 5 (December 1994), same authors.
[59] See for example "EU vetos Deutsche Boerse-London Stock Exchange Merger Deal", *Reuters*, 29/03/2017.

success[60]. It should be noted that execution services react very positively to economies of scale: costs are essentially fixed, whereas revenues are essentially variable.

Paradoxically, all of this ends up fragmenting liquidity: despite numerous mergers and acquisitions, the strong arrival of innovative competitors – particularly in terms of pricing[61] – has created an environment in which there are now many places where it is possible to trade a given instrument. Here is the market share of the main European stock exchanges on some national indices:

	FTSE 100	CAC	DAX	FTSE MIB	IBEX
Primary exchange	London Stock Exchange	Euronext Paris	Xetra	Borsa Italiana	Bolsa de Madrid
Primary market share	58.6%	60.2%	63.2%	72.5%	64.6%
CHIX	19.7%	18.7%	16.4%	13.7%	20.1%
TRQX	12.5%	14.9%	12.3%	5.8%	8.9%
BATS	7.0%	5.2%	6.4%	5.7%	5.5%

CHIX = Chi-X Europe, TRQX = Turquoise, BATS = BATS Europe. These figures represent the component execution market shares of the various exchanges for each index.
Source: LiquidMetrix, a Strategic Insight business, February 2017.

For the United States:

Exchange	Market share
NYSE	24.20%

---

[60] Particularly in the United States and Europe, but Asia-Pacific has also seen similar developments: the Australian authorities blocked the merger of the Sydney and Singapore stock exchanges in 2011. The Tokyo (equities and bonds) and Osaka (derivatives) exchanges merged in 2013.

[61] A traditional stock exchange applies the same pricing structure to a participant who provides liquidity by placing an order in the order book and another who removes liquidity by directly consuming securities at the first limits. One of the fundamental innovations was to *remunerate* liquidity providers. This model is now widely used.

including NYSE Arca	10.50%
BATS	20.90%
including DirectEdge	9.70%
NASDAQ	17.00%
TRFs	37.40%
Other	0.50%
	100%

NYSE (New York Stock Exchange) and Arca (Archipelago Holdings) merged in April 2006. BATS and DirectEdge merged in January 2014. TRFs = trade reporting facilities; these are OTC transactions declared electronically.
Source: author's calculations based on Bloomberg data.

It is still up for debate whether the multiplication of stock exchanges increases absolute liquidity or just fragments it.

3. Post-trade

Post-trade describes all the processes that take place after the protagonists have agreed to transact. Once a transaction is concluded, its solvency is enforced by a clearing house that holds each party responsible, i.e. confirms the details and instructs the necessary transfers. Everyone is obliged to honour these flows under penalty of default, which would result in immediate liquidation of the open positions.

Clearing houses exist for both cash and derivative products, even if the functional cycles are not the same. For a cash product, the central clearer is responsible for the settlement/delivery, i.e. the change of ownership. Typically, this occurs a few days after the initial transaction. In the case of derivatives, the central clearer is responsible for the smooth running of a transaction until the derivative matures, which may be a few days, weeks or even years after the initial transaction. It applies margin calls and an initial margin in all cases, but the characteristics of this collateralisation vary according to the products.

4.   Buy liquidity?

So far, we have focused mainly on equities. This is not just a personal preference; it is also a reflection of the actual market structure of other asset classes. Equities are particularly well suited to fully electronic order book management. They are a segment with a very high presence of individual investors, and the major stock indices are a decent indicator of an economy's strength.

Fixed-income trading does not have the same characteristics. There are few individuals, and the buy-and-hold strategy is prevalent. Take the example of sovereign governments that invest their excess liquidity in foreign currencies. At the end of January 2017, China held $1,051.1 billion in US Treasury bills, notes and bonds, and Japan $1,102.5 billion[62]. The nature of these securities, and their rather institutional use, has had an impact on the speed with which the industry has adopted centralised and electronic trading. There is no fundamental reason why the bond market should be less modern than the equity market, and yet it continues to lag behind. Today, although many sovereign bonds are traded on electronic exchanges, other types of bonds are still traded verbally: a buyer or seller must contact a market maker[63] to obtain a price. To obtain the best price, it is necessary to contact several of them.

Similarly, there is not really a centralised currency market. It is possible to request a price from a large number of participants, often large financial institutions, by telephone or electronically. There are also several purely electronic platforms to which it is relatively easy to connect. Given the small number of currencies to consider and the interconnection of almost all participants, the current structure nevertheless appears efficient[64].

---

[62] *Source*: US Treasury, see: http://ticdata.treasury.gov/Publish/mfh.txt

[63] See Chapter 12 on proprietary trading for a definition and discussion of this term.

[64] Having said that, despite the size of the market and its electronic structure, manipulation has not disappeared. See for example: "Six banks fined $5.6bn over rigging of foreign exchange markets", Financial Times, 20 May 2015.

Generally speaking, the structure of a market – that is, the set of rules that govern trade and allow exchanges to operate – falls into one of two broad categories:

- Some markets are *price-driven*. They are organised around an order book that displays firm prices. Such a book need not be unique; several exchanges can administer one on the same instrument in parallel. Investors looking to buy or sell therefore know at what price they can do so depending on the quantity they are looking for. Price-driven markets are very often electronic from start to finish. Historically, Europe and Asia have evolved along these lines.

- Others are *quote-driven*. This means that an investor seeking liquidity should contact one or more market makers and choose the one that provides the best price. US markets have historically operated on this model, which is the cornerstone of the New York Stock Exchange (where market makers are also called "specialists"). The underlying idea is that the best way for an investor to obtain liquidity is to buy it from a specialised agent, not just publicly display their interest in an order book. The market maker asked for a quote benefits from *de facto* insider information because they are (in theory) the only person who knows that an investor wishes to buy or sell. They can use this information to manage their inventory, and the resulting remuneration is the primary reason for being a market maker[65].

A battle has long raged between these two philosophies, which are still fairly strongly represented across the different asset classes. The regulator has also played a key role in market structures since 2008 to enforce better transparency and efficiency, the ultimate goal being to improve disclosure to end investors and reduce execution costs.

5. Why it matters

---

[65] As we will see, market makers *force themselves* to make a price.

Looking beyond the OTC vs. listed distinction, we are naturally led to an examination of market structures. Broadly speaking, a large majority of cash products are listed nowadays, whereas a large proportion of derivatives are still traded over the counter. But in all cases the modus operandi of the exchanges is fundamentally important since it drives two elements: the dissemination of information and the total cost of execution.

Possessing information can result in immediate gains if you know how to exploit it. Let's say you are one of a few people who happen to have knowledge of an investor who wishes to buy 50,000 shares of a company, at a time when the trading volume is a few thousand shares per day. It is fairly easy to exploit this information: a speculator can pre-emptively rush to buy the securities before the investor, knowing that the price is likely to rise substantially to accommodate demand. Why is that a problem? Because the investor's execution cost becomes higher than it would have been if the speculator had not got wind of the purchase or had been prevented from intervening. The shares purchased by the speculator are no longer available to the investor, meaning they will be forced to pay more for other shares.

Market structure must enforce the greatest possible transparency while eliminating the kind of manipulation described above[66]. If capital markets are to allow an efficient allocation of resources by operating sound supply and demand mechanisms, it is particularly important that intermediaries provide an unbiased service and refrain from exploiting privileged information for their own ends.

---

[66] This particular example is known as front-running and is now liable for criminal prosecution.

XI.   Indexation

1.   What are we talking about?[67]

Before we look at stock market indices, let's consider the fairly similar issue of inflation. How can we intelligently measure changes in consumer prices in an economy? And since we are often required to compare two economies, how can we ensure sufficient homogeneity to enable a fair comparison?

In concrete terms, the following constraints must be addressed:

- *Diversity*: considering only the price of a good or service is too narrow and does not fulfil the mandate. Statisticians therefore devised the household shopping basket, which contains everyday consumer goods (tangible as well as intangible, such as rent or even the lottery).
- *Representativeness*: there is no reason why a French household's basket should be similar to that of a German household, and even less so a Russian one. Comparing them directly makes no sense because their `contents are different; even if there are some common elements, they do not necessarily have the same weighting in the basket, the currency is not the same, etc.
- *Continuity*, i.e. consistency over time: at first glance, the 1970 basket has little in common with the basket of 2017. If there is a change in consumer habits, the sample must evolve and the statistician therefore needs to preserve the continuity of the index.

The indexation principle ticks these boxes simply and elegantly: a statistical institute evaluated a typical basket in 2015, which constitutes the base 100[68]. Every year, the institute collects the prices of the components in this basket and compares them with those of 2015. When the value of the basket has

---

[67] There is a much more complete chapter on this subject in my book *The Complete Arbitrage Deskbook*.

[68] See https://www.insee.fr/fr/metadonnees/definition/c1557 for the exact definition from INSEE in France. The US equivalent is defined by the Bureau of Labor Statistics: https://www.bls.gov/cpi/

increased by 2 points, an index of 102 is published, i.e. inflation is 2%. Moreover, if this methodology is agreed to by the major countries, it becomes possible to compare not just the absolute prices of the different baskets, but their variation over time.

The problem with stock market indices is exactly the same: diversity, representativeness, continuity over time, but also a fourth element, investability, defined as an investor's ability to buy or sell the index[69]. Before we dive a little deeper into the subject, let's take a look at what is already out there.

2. Some well-known indices

The list of stock market indices available on financial information sites is rather long. There are three different types, each of which fulfils different needs:

- *Domestic indices*: CAC 40 (France), DAX (Germany), S&P 500 (US), Nikkei 225 (Japan), FTSE 100 (United Kingdom), FTSE MIB (Italy), IBEX (Spain), etc. These indices contain only domestic companies and are historically the first to have been constructed and published. Before the days of global markets, these indices were used as gauges for national markets. This category also includes indices with smaller companies, called mid caps: SBF 80, FTSE 250, etc.

- *Transnational or regional indices*: Eurostoxx 50, Eurotop 100, MSCI Europe, etc. These indices include stocks from different countries, sometimes from very broad geographical areas. For example, the MSCI World includes securities from all the global exchanges.

- *Sector indices*: Nasdaq 100 in the United States, all STOXX sector indices in Europe (SX7E and SX7P for the banking industry). As their name suggests, these indices combine stocks from the same sector, allowing investors to refine their choices and not be exposed to an entire economy.

---

[69] This is not necessary for inflation: being able to physically buy the Japanese household basket is of little interest.

The table below provides a broad overview of what exists around the world:

(as of Feb. 14, 2017)	Country / zone	Closing Price	Currency	Nb Const.	Type	Description	Weighting	Base	Date	Mkt Cap (billions $)
CAC 40	France	4,888.19	EUR	40	D	Large Cap	C	1,000	31-déc.-87	$1,562.84
SBF 120	France	3,873.77	EUR	119	D	Large & Mid Cap	C	1,000	28-déc.-90	$2,116.75
DAX	Germany	11,774.43	EUR	30	D	Large Cap	C DivR	1,000	31-déc.-87	$1,276.03
MDAX	Germany	23,250.38	EUR	50	D	Mid Cap	C DivR	1,000	31-déc.-87	$386.03
AEX	Netherlands	494.05	EUR	25	D	Large Cap	C DivR	538.36	4-janv.-99	$673.22
IBEX 35	Spain	9,484.10	EUR	35	D	Large Cap	C	3,000	29-déc.-89	$674.41
SMI	Switzerland	8,462.88	CHF	20	D	Large Cap	C	1,500	30-juin-88	$1,147.75
FTSE MIB	Italy	19,064.64	EUR	40	D	Large Cap	C		30-déc.-83	$479.10
FTSE 100	UK	7,278.92	GBP	101	D	Large Cap	C	1,000	30-déc.-83	$2,639.29
FTSE 250	UK	18,758.78	GBP	250	D	Mid & Small Cap	C	1,412.60	31-déc.-85	$513.05
Eurostoxx 50	Europe	3,305.23	EUR	50	D	Large Cap Zone Euro	C			$3,128.64
Stoxx 50	Europe	3,058.95	EUR	50	MN	Large Cap	C			$4,461.00
Stoxx 600	Europe	370.13	EUR	600	MN	Large & Mid Cap	C	1,000		$11,043.98
MSCI Europe	Europe	125.31	EUR	446	MN	Large & Mid Cap	C	100	31-déc.-98	$10,685.29
MICEX	Russia	2,161.49	RUB	50	D	Large Cap	C	100	22-sept.-97	$614.83
S&P 500	US	2,328.25	USD	505	D	Large & Mid Cap	C	10	1941-1943	$22,322.88
Dow Jones	US	20,412.16	USD	30	D	Large Cap	E		1-oct.-28	$6,236.84
Russell 3000	US	1,385.27	USD	2,965	D	Large, Mid & Small	C	125	1-févr.-85	$27,866.83
Nasdaq 100	US	5,256.82	USD	107	D	Techno Large Cap	C	125	1-févr.-85	$6,632.67
Nasdaq Composite	US	5,763.96	USD	2,548	D	Techno Large, Mid & Small	C	100	5-févr.-71	$9,652.72
BOVESPA	Brazil	66,967.64	BRL	59	D	Large Cap	C			$726.58
S&P TSX 60	Canada	929.68	CAD	60	D	Large Cap	C			$1,371.40
IPC	Mexico	47,661.69	MXN	35	D	Large Cap	C	0.78	30-oct.-78	$291.27
Nikkei 225	Japan	19,459.15	JPY	225	D	Large Cap	S	176.21	16-mai-49	$3,308.53
TOPIX	Japan	1,554.20	JPY	1,999	D	Large, Mid & Small	C	100	4-janv.-68	$5,518.43
S&P ASX 200	Australia	5,760.69	AUD	200	D	Large Cap	C			$1,365.12
HSI	Hong-Kong	23,710.98	HKD	50	D	Large Cap	C	100	31-juil.-64	$2,067.11
CSI 300	China	3,436.28	CNY	300	D	Large Cap	C	1,000	31-déc.-04	$3,804.45
Shanghai Composite	China	3,216.84	CNY	1,246	D	Large, Mid & Small	C	100	19-déc.-90	$4,684.50
Shenzhen Composite	China	1,964.75	CNY	1,941	D	Large, Mid & Small	C	100	3-avr.-91	$3,590.48
TAIEX	Taiwan	9,710.32	TWD	870	D	Large, Mid & Small	C	100	1966	$996.83
FTSE TWSE 50	Taiwan	7,295.74	TWD	50	D	Large Cap	C	5,000	30-avr.-02	$684.53
KOSPI 200	South Korea	268.81	KRW	200	D	Large, Mid Cap	C	100	3-janv.-90	$1,078.35
KOSPI	South Korea	2,078.65	KRW	767	D	Large, Mid & Small	C	100	4-janv.-80	$1,220.28
NIFTY 50	India	8,805.05	INR	51	D	Large, Mid & Small	C			$977.56
S&P BSE 500	India	12,048.60	INR	501	D	Large, Mid & Small	C	1,000	1-févr.-99	$1,723.64
FTSE Straits	Singapore	3,111.63	SGD	30	D	Large Cap	C			$377.77
LQ45	Indonesia	900.72	IDR	45	D	Large Cap	C	100	13-juil.-94	$314.86

Legend:

- D = domestic, MN = multinational;
- Nb Const. = number of constituents;
- base = reference value on the index's first calculation day, date = first calculation date;
- C = capitalisation, C DivR = capitalisation with reinvestment of dividends, P = price, E = equal-weighted;
- Mkt Cap = total market capitalisation of the index, i.e. the sum of all the individual capitalisations;
- Currency = quotation currency, EUR = euro, CHF = Swiss franc, GBP = British pound, USD = US dollar, RUB = Russian rouble, BRL = Brazilian real, CAD = Canadian dollar, MXN = Mexican peso, AUD = Australian dollar, JPY = yen, HKG = Hong Kong dollar, CNY = Chinese yuan, TWD = Taiwan dollar, KRW = Korean won, INR = Indian rupee, SGD = Singapore dollar, IDR = Indonesian rupee.

These different indices can be used in several ways: investors will follow the particular index that suits their needs, depending on whether they are interested in a country, a region or a sector. This index can then serve as a benchmark. For example, if an investor decides to acquire units in a mutual fund specialising in commodities, they could easily compare the manager's performance to a sector index to determine whether the fund has added value or it would be preferable to invest directly in the index. We will come back to this later.

The way in which an index is defined, its constituents and the rigour of its methodology are very important because it aggregates a vast array of information to then display it in condensed form. Historically, national stock exchanges (Euronext, Deutsche Börse, London Stock Exchange) were responsible for maintaining domestic indices. Today, most of the major indices, i.e. those used predominantly by institutional investors, are the property of the commercial companies that design and operate them: STOXX, MSCI or FTSE Russell for example[70].

What does "operate" mean here? Typically, index sponsors guarantee, through their research and knowledge of the markets, that the indices they publish meet the requirements we have mentioned: diversity, representativeness, continuity and investability. Investors can then benefit from this expertise in several ways:

- By acquiring data on a daily basis, which makes it possible to build an exact replica portfolio or a near replica one by, for example, slightly changing the weightings or eliminating a country or sector;
- By purchasing the right to use the name and performance. For example, a bank wishing to issue and distribute a product indexed to the Eurostoxx 50 or the MSCI Europe will have to acquire from STOXX or MSCI a licence on their intellectual property, i.e. the right to reference the index and to use its name in addition to its constitution.

Sponsors are therefore looking for renown, which is reflected in the mass of savings managed using their indices as benchmarks. For example, MSCI announced $2,500 billion in assets indexed to its MSCI World indices at the end of June 2016 (https://www.msci.com/world). However, although the sponsor is the custodian of the operating rules (components, weighting methodology, etc.), it is not always technically responsible for calculating its own indices. This task generally falls to stock exchanges. They are in fact the only ones in a position to know the real-time prices of each component and to electronically publish the corresponding index level.

---

[70] See https://www.stoxx.com/, https://www.msci.com/, http://www.ftserussell.com/. Please forgive my bias towards equities. The same logic applies to other asset classes; there are of course bond, currency, commodity indices, etc.

3. Calculation

How is an index calculated in practice? Take an index with a base of 100 set on 15 January 2015, comprising three shares: A, B and C. Suppose the weights of each are $W_A = 1$, $W_B = 3$, $W_C = 5$. The value of the index I today is:

$$I = 100 \times \left(\frac{W_A \times P_A + W_B \times P_B + W_C \times P_C}{W_A \times P_A^0 + W_B \times P_B^0 + W_C \times P_C^0} \right) = 100 \times \left(\frac{P_A + 3 \times P_B + 5 \times P_C}{P_A^0 + 3 \times P_B^0 + 5 \times P_C^0} \right)$$

where:

- P_A, P_B, P_C = share prices for A, B and C today
- P_A^0, P_B^0, P_C^0 = the prices of A, B and C on January 15, 2015

If I is worth 110 today and has been correctly constructed in terms of diversity and representativeness, we can deduce that the *market* has gained 10% between January 2015 and today[71].

Which raises the question: how do you choose the constituents and their weights W? What happens if the weight has changed since 15 January 2015? Do we want the index to reflect this change as well, in addition to the price change?

In accordance with the principles set out above, the underlying basket of a stock index must be representative and diversified according to a given objective. If the intention is to follow a domestic market, as many national companies as possible should be included. If the goal is to measure the performance of a sector, we will restrict ourselves to that sector, etc. It soon becomes clear, however, that few economies are deep enough to offer a wide choice of liquid securities, especially when filtering by industry. Hence the birth of transnational indices, particularly in Europe where national champions conduct a lot of their business abroad.

---

[71] By definition, I is a dimensionless quantity, being the ratio of two numbers that have the same unit ($). If someone says the S&P 500 is at $2,316, it is therefore a mistake. The S&P stands at 2,316 *points*; these points are not a currency unit.

The weights are generally fixed according to one of two methodologies[72]:

- In the vast majority of cases, W is the total number of shares outstanding. We will see below why these indices are described as capitalisation-weighted;
- Some indices are weighted simply and equally for all stocks (Dow Jones and Nikkei 225). Those are called price-weighted indices.

To understand the difference between these two approaches, let's return to the index A, B, C above and change the price of A by an amount d_A: A becomes $(A + d_A)$. The change in the value of I is d_I: I becomes $(I + d_I)$. It is fairly easy to show that[73]:

$$\frac{d_I}{I} = \left(\frac{W_A \times P_A}{C}\right) \times \left(\frac{d_A}{P_A}\right)$$

where $C = W_A \times P_A + W_B \times P_B + W_C \times P_C$: this quantity is the total market capitalisation since $W_A \times P_A$ = (number of shares outstanding x share price) is the capitalisation of company A. All this means the variation of the index (dI/I) is proportional to the variation of A (dA/A), and the proportionality coefficient is none other than the relative capitalisation of A. Hence, why these are known as cap-weighted indices.

If for example:

- A represents 10% of the market capitalisation: $W_A \times P_A / C = 10\%$.
- A goes from $100 to $105: dA = $5, dA/PA = 5/100 = 5%

the result is that I moves by 0.5%: $dI/I = 10\% \times 5\% = 0.5\%$.

This is to be contrasted with a simple weighting, e.g. equal weighting of A, B and C. In this case: $W_A = W_B = W_C = 1$ and:

---

[72] The same methodologies are used for bond indices. For currency indices, the situation is slightly different: the notion of capitalisation is meaningless, so we often use simple weighted indices, i.e. equally weighted.

[73] This is a differential calculation identical to the one discussed in the chapter on risk analysis.

$$\frac{W_A \times P_A}{C} = \frac{P_A}{P_A + P_B + P_C}$$

The impact of a variation of A on I is therefore proportional to the relative price of A compared with the other constituents of I. This simply means that a stock with a high price will have a high impact on the index, even if its capitalisation is low[74].

In the case of Nikkei and Dow Jones, all members have equal weight, so the impact of a stock's movement depends on its relative price. Put another way, two companies with the same price have the same impact. The result is sometimes surprising: the Nikkei 225 contains huge corporations as well as much smaller companies, and yet their impact on the index will be similar if their stock prices are.

4. Generalisation

Following on from the above, here is the generic formula for a stock index:

$$I = \frac{W_1 \times P_1 + W_2 \times P_2 + \cdots + W_n \times P_n}{D}$$

where: W_i = the weight of security i, P_i = the price of security i, D = divisor, n = number of constituents, for example 500 in the case of the S&P 500. We will come back to the definition of the divisor and its usefulness a little later.

This formula can be written differently:

$$I = \left(\frac{W_1}{D}\right) \times P_1 + \left(\frac{W_2}{D}\right) \times P_2 + \cdots + \left(\frac{W_n}{D}\right) \times P_n$$
$$= Q_1 \times P_1 + Q_2 \times P_2 + \cdots + Q_n \times P_n$$

where Q_i = (W_i/D). In this formula, I is (also) the value of a portfolio consisting of Q_i shares of each security i. Put another way, if you took a

---

[74] NB: the price of a stock has nothing to do with its capitalisation: a company whose stock has a very low price could have an enormous capitalisation, and vice versa.

portfolio with a quantity Q_i of each stock, its value would always equal that of the index. The table below shows the French CAC 40:

Constituent	Weight	Closing 2/13/17	Quantity (100 indices)	Capitalisation (millions €)
TOTAL SA	2,377.97	48.08 €	1,087	€ 114,321
Sanofi	1,160.11	80.38 €	530	€ 93,250
BNP Paribas SA	1,121.82	56.35 €	512	€ 63,214
LVMH Moet Hennessy Louis Vuitton SE	279.25	189.80 €	127	€ 53,002
AXA SA	1,939.38	23.01 €	886	€ 44,616
L'Oreal SA	251.90	173.70 €	115	€ 43,755
Air Liquide SA	388.60	103.25 €	177	€ 40,123
Airbus SE	579.51	65.85 €	264	€ 38,161
Vinci SA	536.04	69.36 €	245	€ 37,180
Schneider Electric SE	532.55	68.62 €	243	€ 36,544
Danone SA	590.30	60.65 €	269	€ 35,802
Societe Generale SA	767.27	42.77 €	350	€ 32,812
Orange SA	1,995.04	14.41 €	912	€ 28,739
Nokia OYJ	5,835.56	4.64 €	2,668	€ 27,071
LafargeHolcim Ltd	455.18	52.98 €	208	€ 24,116
Cie de Saint-Gobain	499.41	46.43 €	228	€ 23,185
Pernod Ricard SA	212.34	108.95 €	97	€ 23,134
Essilor International SA	207.19	109.45 €	94	€ 22,677
Unibail-Rodamco SE	99.32	218.40 €	45	€ 21,691
Safran SA	312.77	64.32 €	142	€ 20,118
Cie Generale des Etablissements Michelin	182.27	104.00 €	83	€ 18,957
Engie SA	1,582.94	11.31 €	723	€ 17,903
Kering	75.77	232.00 €	34	€ 17,578
ArcelorMittal	1,992.71	8.62 €	911	€ 17,169
Vivendi SA	964.96	17.27 €	441	€ 16,660
Renault SA	177.43	87.50 €	81	€ 15,525
Legrand SA	267.07	54.09 €	122	€ 14,446
Valeo SA	238.39	58.86 €	108	€ 14,031
Credit Agricole SA	1,123.72	11.58 €	513	€ 13,013
Publicis Groupe SA	203.18	63.62 €	92	€ 12,927
Capgemini SA	163.57	78.09 €	74	€ 12,773
Carrefour SA	529.36	22.78 €	242	€ 12,059
Sodexo SA	92.24	102.60 €	42	€ 9,464
Peugeot SA	485.17	17.93 €	221	€ 8,697
Solvay SA	74.11	113.10 €	33	€ 8,382
Klepierre	220.05	35.66 €	100	€ 7,847
Veolia Environnement SA	478.86	16.25 €	218	€ 7,781
Bouygues SA	207.27	34.64 €	94	€ 7,180
Accor SA	170.82	38.94 €	78	€ 6,652
TechnipFMC PLC	220.21	30.00 €	100	€ 6,606
Capitalisation (millions €)		1,069,159.57 €	487,413 €	
Divisor		218.722819		
CAC		4,888.194		

Sources: author's calculations and Bloomberg data.

For Total, for example, the weight represents the number of shares outstanding - 2,377.97 (million). By virtue of the above, if we calculate:

$$Q = \frac{W}{D} = \frac{2\,377{,}97}{218{,}722819} = 10{,}872$$

the divisor is the denominator of the index. As we will see later, it captures and neutralises all changes in the index that are not due to price movements.

We obtain the number of Total shares in 1 CAC index, i.e. 10.872, or 1,087 per 100 indices, after rounding down. The total capitalisation of the CAC is €1,069.16 billion, and that of the basket is €487,413[75,76].

This somewhat boring arithmetic has a virtue: it gives meaning to the expression *buy the CAC index*, namely buying all the constituents in proportion to what is necessary to reproduce the index, i.e. the Q_i above. It is this "underlying index ⇔ basket" correspondence that forms the basis of the notion of investability. If the basket is clearly and intelligently defined, the index can be easily bought or sold, thus manufacturing an economic exposure to what the index represents. Conversely, if it is difficult to buy because the constituents are illiquid, or if the operating rules are not clear, investors will look elsewhere for an index that is easier to replicate.

5. Active or passive management?

In the world of mutualised asset management, indexation is an increasingly popular technique. As mentioned above, the existence of a large number of indices, categorised by region or theme, gives substance to the idea that it is possible to measure "the tide and not the waves". Moreover, when those indices are well designed, it is easy to reproduce their behaviour.

So any investor, retail or institutional, is faced with the following choice: for a given target – e.g. the technology sector in the US – should I entrust my capital to an experienced but expensive – fees are typically between 1.5% and 2% per year – fund manager, or should I seek to reproduce the behaviour of a carefully chosen index (e.g. the Nasdaq 100)? Managers offer an active management service, i.e. they will pick the securities and more generally build the portfolio according to their convictions, themselves based on the

[75] This total capitalisation figure for the CAC 40 is significantly different from the one shown in the table in Section 2 of this chapter because the number of shares used is different. Here, in the *actual* composition of the CAC, we consider only the "free float" number of shares, not the total number of shares issued. EDF is a classic case, even if it is not in the CAC 40: a large part of the equity is in the hands of the French government and does not circulate, meaning it is excluded from the free float.
[76] If the CAC is at 4,888.19, 100 CACs must be 488,819. The difference with 487,413 is due to rounding off the (integer) quantity for each constituent.

managers' research and analysis; in passive management, investors are happy to simply replicate the behaviour of an index, which is far cheaper[77].

Conscious of this new environment, the asset management industry has therefore developed dedicated passive management products: index funds and exchange traded funds (ETFs). These are still investment funds, but their fundamental characteristics differ from those of other mutual funds:

- The objective of an index fund is, as its name indicates, explicit and simple: to exactly replicate the benchmark index. There is no stock-picking and no analysis. The manager is literally reduced to a passive replication function. Of course, given the nature of the service, the management company's remuneration is much less than for active management.

- An ETF has the same management objective, with the additional characteristic of being listed on an exchange. This means a price is available at any time for anyone who wants to place an order[78]. In contrast, traditional mutual funds or trust units are not listed. To buy or sell them, an instruction must be sent to the centralising agent, who will forward it to the management company responsible for the fund (the transaction is typically confirmed at closing prices, only once a day). The world's biggest ETF is the SPDR (pronounced "spider" S&P 500 in the US, with approximately $157 billion of assets and a management fee of 0.09%. Anyone who has ever invested in mutual funds knows that 0.09% is a *very* competitive fee.

To return to the initial question, the investor's choice therefore comes down to this:

- Should I pay for the expertise of a manager in the hope they will outperform the benchmark index, bearing in mind they can underperform as well as outperform?

---

[77] For various reasons, replicating a bond index is more difficult than replicating an equity index. The price of passive management therefore varies greatly depending on the asset class, but it is still much cheaper than active management.
[78] In addition, the number of market makers is often high (see the chapter on proprietary trading and management on behalf of third parties).

- Or should I choose an index fund or ETF that will precisely replicate the benchmark's performance, but at a low cost[79]?

It is up to everyone to position themselves according to their convictions, but I have a few things to say, if I may. Almost all fund managers chronically underperform their benchmark. This is not speculation; it is a very well documented fact. It is even the subject of institutional statistical studies, for example in the US by Standard and Poor's, which has developed a methodology called SPIVA (S&P Indices Versus Active) to examine this question[80]. Here is one of the conclusions of the study published at the end of June 2016:

"During the one-year period, 84.62% of large-cap managers, 87.89% of mid-cap managers, and 88.77% of small-cap managers underperformed the S&P 500, the S&P MidCap 400®, and the S&P SmallCap 600®, respectively".

This is by no means an exceptional result. Over a five-year period, these figures rise to 91.91%, 87.87% and 97.58%.

So it is no surprise that ETFs are growing very rapidly in the US, and therefore worldwide. Indexing and its practical manifestation – passive management – have become major phenomena. Index sponsors therefore take great care to maintain a varied and relevant product mix, now including a genuine passive element.

---

[79] At the risk of stating the obvious, management fees are deducted directly from the fund, thus having an immediate impact on performance. All other things being equal, a fund that charges 1.5% per annum will underperform by 1% each year a fund that charges only 0.5%.

[80] See for example http://us.spindices.com/documents/spiva/spiva-us-mid-year-2016.pdf for the mid-2016 report and http://us.spindices.com/documents/research/research-spiva-institutional-scorecard-how-much-do-fees-affect-the-active-versus-passive-debate.pdf for a discussion on the impact of fees on the active/passive debate.

6.   A word on continuity

So far, we have deftly avoided the issue of recomposition. What happens if a stock leaves one index and is replaced by another? Let's consider the following situation: today, I consists of (A, B, C); tomorrow morning, C is replaced by D:

$$I_{before} = \frac{W_A \times P_A + W_B \times P_B + W_C \times P_C}{D}$$

$$I_{after} = \frac{W_A \times P_A + W_B \times P_B + W_D \times P_D}{D}$$

Prices have been kept constant because this has happened outside market hours, i.e. *after closing* today and *before opening* tomorrow. We are interested in the structural variation of the index, distinct from a price variation.

The two expressions can be equal only if $W_C \times P_C = W_D \times P_D$, which in real life has no reason to be the case. C and D are different companies and there is no reason they would have the same capitalisation. On the other hand, it would be annoying if I_{before} and I_{after} were different. If the S&P 500 is at 4,800 this evening, it is also at 4,800 tomorrow morning, otherwise it does not measure what it is supposed to measure: a variation in the prices, and only the prices, of its constituents. If the continuity of I is forced from one day to the next, something must be adjusted and this adjustment is found in the divisor:

$$I_{before} = \frac{W_A \times P_A + W_B \times P_B + W_C \times P_C}{D} = I_{after}$$
$$= \frac{W_A \times P_A + W_B \times P_B + W_D \times P_D}{D'}$$

D reflects the increase or decrease in total index capitalisation that is not due to a price change:

$$D' = D \times \left(\frac{W_A \times P_A + W_B \times P_B + W_D \times P_D}{W_A \times P_A + W_B \times P_B + W_C \times P_C} \right)$$

$$= D \times \frac{Total\ Capitalisation\ After}{Total\ Capitalisation\ Before}$$

What is true for a securities substitution is also true for a large number of common operations: reinvested dividends, rights or new share issues, delistings, stock splits, etc. This can be summarised as follows: stock indices are *adjusted* (via their divisor) for changes in the capital structure of their components, so their variation is immune to these changes in order to capture only price changes. Q.E.D.

7. Why it matters

Hopefully, this somewhat lengthy tour of indexation has helped to clarify matters. I included this chapter for three reasons.

First, stock market indices have undeniably become the yardstick for the health of global financial markets. The media routinely report the performance of the Dow Jones, the Nikkei, the Eurostoxx, etc. without any explanation of what these figures represent, or of the general idea that has led to the creation of a growing number of diverse and varied indices. No more excuses for you, I'm afraid: you now know what the S&P 500 represents, what makes it move and to what extent.

Secondly, we need to acknowledge the vast numbers of indices out there today. The big sponsors offer a huge array for developed and developing economies, regions, industries, etc. This extensive choice makes it possible to find a benchmark for almost any trading strategy. If tomorrow you met a trader selling his/her expertise in Asian biotechs, you could find an index on the same theme in less than an hour. From there, you can easily determine whether the trader's strategy is really adding value.

All the above creates a dilemma that we referred to earlier and is increasingly common for institutional and retail investors alike: what type of management for what price/performance ratio? It's the chicken and the egg. Has the chronic underperformance of active management led to more indices being created, thereby causing a shift towards index and other similar funds? Or has the extensive index offering pushed more and more investors towards indexing?

Whatever the answer, the end result is irrefutable, as shown in Figures 11.1 and 11.2. The first displays the equity fund market share of index funds (in the US, but the same applies everywhere), and the second shows the relative growth of ETF assets compared with the industry as a whole (base 1 in 2003).

Figure 11.1 - *Index funds (% market share of equity funds, US)*

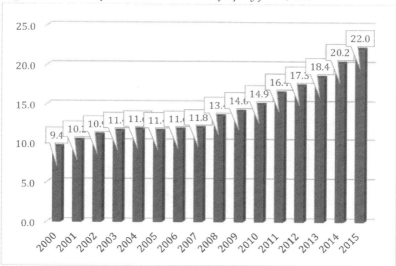

Figure 11.2 - *Relative growth in ETF and mutual fund AuM*

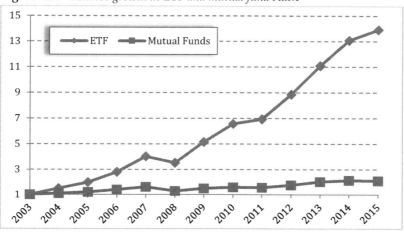

Source: Investment Company Institute Factbook 2016, www.ici.org.

At the end of 2015, index funds accounted for 22% of all equity fund assets, more than doubling over 15 years. Over the period 2003-2015, ETF assets under management (AuM) increased fourteen-fold, while those of mutual funds merely doubled.

The answer to the question is therefore as follows: indexing is important because it is the future of collective asset management and therefore of end investors' demand for services from trading floors.

XII.   Asset management and proprietary trading

1.   What are we talking about?

It is essential to be able to distinguish between the different types of economic agents likely to intervene on the capital markets. Each entity's purpose, intervention methods, ability to take and assume risk over time, and regulatory regime all condition their behaviour and require them to be categorised.

At the risk of minor broad brushing, there are seven such categories:

- *Large corporates* are commercial companies whose size justifies and enables direct participation. Intervening *directly* on the market presupposes a couple of conditions: (i) the necessary human and artificial intelligence to understand products, control risks and master modelling; (ii) transactions big enough to warrant intervention in a wholesale market. It is hard to imagine a local bakery contacting a multinational for its supplies. Even though the internet has shaken things up, distribution networks in almost all industries have been structured according to customer size: wholesale, semi-wholesale, retail, etc. The structure is identical in finance. A company often uses an intermediary, typically a bank, to access certain products or services, or to hedge certain risks.

- *Insurance companies* have specific needs related to their operational cycle. An insurer receives predictable and regular premiums from its clients and must deal with unpredictable and irregular outflows, i.e. the reimbursement of claims. The money collected must therefore be invested in products whose risk profile is adapted to the inherent macroeconomic risk, all within a binding regulatory framework. For example, it is reasonable to assume that, over time, a car insurer will have different needs to one specialising in natural disasters.

- *Asset management companies* aim to grow the savings entrusted to them by their clients. These clients include pension funds, large corporate accounts, sovereign wealth funds, private individuals, etc. Asset managers are usually separated into two subcategories according to their degree of regulation, and consequently their appetite for risk: long-only and hedge funds. The long-only category includes the most regulated players, for whom risk is often upside exposure to cash assets, typically equities and bonds. Derivatives and leverage are rarely used[81]. The other category comprises the more speculative hedge funds, which can be marketed only to qualified investors almost all over the world[82]. Hedge funds have a much broader mandate and are generally not subject to any regulation. They are therefore frequent users of derivatives on all kinds of asset classes[83].

- *Investment banks,* often referred to by the acronym CIB (corporate and investment banks), are the main players. They carry out transactions for their own account, as well as on behalf of their clients, to cover their own risk and that of their clients.
- *Central banks,* which are mainly active in currencies and interest rates, are responsible for monetary stability[84].
- *Exchanges* work very specifically to ensure that transactions between participants are as transparent as possible. Exchanges may list cash products, derivatives or both.
- *Independent brokers* are financial institutions specialising in intermediation. Rarely in a position to incur risk for their own account due to a lack of equity capital, their role is to facilitate exchanges, just as a real estate broker's function is to bring buyers and sellers together without actually taking part in the transaction.

---

[81] An investor who buys a product hoping for an upside gain is "long" of the market. The opposite sell position is a "short". A well-functioning economy leads to growth in the value of its assets over the medium term. This is why, for many investors, going long is much more natural than going short.

[82] For example, even in the US, where most hedge funds are domiciled, only accredited investors can invest in them. An accredited investor is an individual whose wealth exceeds $1,000,000 or whose income has exceeded $200,000 in each of the past two years.

[83] It should be stressed that hedge funds account for only a small part of collective AuM: at the end of 2015, over $37 trillion were invested in long-only funds, vs. only around $2.7 trillion in hedge funds.

[84] There are some special cases. Japan's central bank, for example, does not hesitate to buy shares directly to support the Nikkei when it deems it necessary.

For our purposes, we will focus here on two of these categories: asset management companies – understood as either long-only or hedge funds – and investment banks.

There are real similarities between the two: the degree of sophistication in understanding products and risks is limited only by the means deployed, as opposed to a company like Apple whose legitimacy to invest, for example, in emerging-market bonds is questionable[85]. Moreover, both categories have a mandate to use this sophistication to serve a performance objective: growing clients' savings on the one hand and the bank's own funds on the other. There is a common interest there. As a result, asset managers and CIBs should be, and are, the main market participants, particularly in derivatives.

Despite those similarities, there are currently at least two fundamental reasons why the behaviour of these two categories is mutually exclusive, even if this has not always been the case:
- incentives, i.e. the remuneration of managers and traders;
- regulation, which eliminated the notion of "proprietary trading" in banks.

Let's take a closer look.

2. Mandate and remuneration

In most asset managers and banks, operators have quantified targets for the value they create and the performance of their positions. But how is this performance measured?

An investment fund, in the broadest sense, works as follows. A group of investors collects a given sum, for example $100, on the basis of a management strategy that they believe is sound, profitable and adapted to the market environment. For example, investing in biotechnology

---

[85] And yet: Apple has a huge cash reserve, estimated at over $200 billion. This mountain of cash is invested in what is *de facto* the world's largest hedge fund: Braeburn Capital. See for example: https://en.wikipedia.org/wiki/Braeburn_Capital.

companies in the developed economies of Europe, the US and Japan. This strategy will be set in motion by a manager, who should be able to analyse and choose the appropriate instruments and manage the risks. If investors find that their units/shares are worth $105 after 1 year (i.e. a performance of 5%), they are entitled to wonder if this gain represents real added value or if the manager was just lucky. After all, the manager might have chosen the right instruments for the wrong reasons or, conversely, missed opportunities that would have engendered a much higher return. As investors are by no means experts on the subject, it is impossible for them to validate every trading decision. If they were, why would they employ a third-party manager?

This raises the question of the manager's remuneration. On the one hand, a fixed remuneration allows the manager to work and pay for premises and sources of information such as real-time data flows, etc. For these fixed costs, the asset manager charges "management fees", typically between 1.5% and 2.5%, which are deducted from AuM[86]. On the other hand, to align everyone's interests, investors will want the manager to be paid according to performance. This variable part of the remuneration is called the *performance* fee. Typically, it amounts to 20%: on a gain of $5, the manager will take $1 and leave only $4 for share/unitholders.

This situation makes assessing the manager all the more important: if a performance fee is to be paid, it might as well be for genuine outperformance. That is why we use a benchmark, typically a well-known index. In the case mentioned above, it could be a biotech index calculated by a well-established sponsor. Comparing the fund's 5% gain with the performance of the benchmark gives a good idea of the *true* value added by the manager.

To summarise, here is a reasonable framework for aligning the manager's and your interests:
- choose a manager and a benchmark;

---

[86] The operating costs of a management company are fixed; its income depends on assets under management. Look no further for the reason why the industry has always been a race for assets.

- negotiate a dual remuneration structure: management fees for day-to-day operations, performance fees for extras;
- regularly compare the performance of the fund with its benchmark to assess the validity of the investment. Potentially change managers or opt for a passive version, i.e. one in which the fund directly replicates the index[87].

None of this applies to a trader in a bank. When an operator sets up at their desk, they have no capital to manage. All the positions they take are financed from their employer's own funds. In practice, this means that a fund manager wishing to buy a security does not have to borrow the necessary amount because the money has already been paid by investors, whereas a bank trader must call the central treasury and check under what conditions they can finance their inventory – and of course what their limits are. In fact, they will have checked all these parameters with management on arrival. They must *always* borrow the cash they need and pay interest on it. On the other hand, although their acceptable risks and eligible products and markets are dictated to them, they are not subject to a benchmark comparison. Their pay is therefore dependent not on relative performance but on the total gains identified as a result of their trading. Since risk and profitability are proportional, an operator in a bank has very good reasons to incur risk.

All this leads to significantly different behaviour:
- Since they are compared with a benchmark, asset managers are not sensitive to an absolute level of risk, only a relative one. If, for example, lacking conviction, they fall back on their benchmark index and temporarily replicate its composition, their performance will not be better, but it will not be worse either. Put another way, they have no *fundamental* reason to take on risk. Traders are in a completely different situation: whatever their strategy, they will have to cover their costs, including financing. In addition to the service they provide to their clients, their mandate naturally encourages them to take risks because it is the only way they can

---

[87] In this case, as the process is passive and largely automated, it is easy to negotiate lower costs.

produce results. Simply put, managers who merely replicate their benchmark will not be sanctioned for that because they will have fulfilled their mandate. Traders who fail to cover their direct and indirect costs (financing, etc.) will soon find themselves out of a job.

- Asset managers have little need for debt. In theory, they manage their leverage by refinancing their positions[88], but in practice this is not really in their interests because the amount would be limited by the assets at their disposal. For traders, however, debt and leverage are intrinsic to their work. Although bound by balance sheet and risk constraints, they are free to trade what they want in the volume they want. If, for example, managers detect an excellent opportunity to earn 0.10%, they will probably be able to seize it on only part of the available capital. Traders, on the other hand, could potentially convince management to deploy substantial capital, particularly if the gain can be realised in the near future.

- Managers are basically at the service of their clients: no clients, no assets to manage. Their primary function is to *manage on behalf of a third party*. The situation is quite different for traders: faced with limited resources, they can choose to allocate risk to a transaction initiated by them or by a client. They have a mandate to *manage for their own account*, also known as proprietary trading, and are responsible for putting some of their resources at their clients' disposal.

In a bank, the macroeconomic result is as follows: market risk and leverage depend essentially on addressable opportunities and therefore, to a certain extent, on the remuneration structure of the operators, which is proportionate with risk.

At least, that was how it worked before the 2008 crisis changed everything.

---

[88] See Chapter 13 on (re)financing.

3.   Market making

The presentation to this point reflects the world view that the media has churned out since 2008. How soon we forget that the crisis – initially in real estate – was rooted in widespread speculation, particularly in the US. Banks certainly facilitated contagion, but they were far from being the root cause.

In response, regulators asked themselves the following question: how can we control the level of risk taken by large investment banks, knowing that: (i) an intrinsic mechanism rewards risk-taking on trading floors; and (ii) if banks are no longer able to take risks, who will provide prices to clients, particularly asset managers, who desperately need financial engineering to manage their own risks?

The idea that has emerged is to split portfolios into two parts: one for clients and one for everything else (mainly proprietary trading), this latter part being considered at best useless and at worst harmful because it generates additional risk. It is the equivalent of capping power on motorcycles: going beyond a certain speed is pointless and perhaps even dangerous. Moreover, putting your foot down is justified only if a client has *explicitly* asked you to. It's a useful analogy: advocates of capping a motorbike's power will tell you it is for public safety, in the same way that banking regulation aims to bring about collective financial stability.

I'm not here to argue whether this is right or wrong, but there is something I can contribute to the debate in the form of a variation on the hot potato metaphor. If the size of the potato represents an absolute level of risk (which is unpredictable because it is random), sound risk management is not about looking for someone who will be stuck with the potato, but rather agreeing on a way to cut it up and distribute the pieces to as many people as possible as quickly as possible, in the hope of limiting individual burns while the pieces cool. The more people are excluded from the group, the harder it is to cope with large hot potatoes. Similarly, over time, preventing individual banks from incurring risk significantly reduces the total risk that the economy can bear.

The solution adopted by regulators involves the advent of "market making"[89]. This refers to an activity in which a trader makes a market for a client on a given product. Making a market involves simultaneously providing a purchase and a sale price for minimum quantities. The client can then carry out the transaction at a known price or refuse it. Most national legislations impose this idea and prohibit proprietary activities for financial institutions.[90] Only market making is authorised. Traders are therefore extremely constrained in their interventions: it is illegal to carry out a transaction that is not justified by a client interest or by hedging an existing risk.

The term market making refers to codified economic behaviour, as opposed to a product or technique. For example, if you are a regular wheat buyer, it is reassuring to know you will always find a seller who will show a price. In the automotive industry, the market maker is a dealer who has to make a trade-in offer on your used car, regardless of its make, condition or mileage. At the same time, the dealer will also be able to provide you with a price for any of the vehicles in his/her showroom.

It is obviously reassuring to buy a vehicle you know you will be able to sell at any time. The price might not be competitive or as high as you had hoped, but it's better than no price at all. The more standardised the good or service, the easier it is to monetise, i.e. the lower the risk is for market makers because they will find it easier to sell the good or service on. That is why there is no natural market maker in real estate.

Imposed by regulation in the wake of the 2008 crisis, the market maker has become a very important concept in finance. Traders in large institutions are required to display prices on a fairly wide range of derivative and non-derivative products, and they collect a margin or commission for each transaction:

- Anyone looking to buy a share in company ABC will naturally turn to institutions that have declared themselves to be market makers on that stock. This gives them a better chance of finding an

---

[89] Regulators have also sought to limit the remuneration of "risk-taking" personnel.
[90] In France, see Article 2 of Act No. 2013-672 of 26 July 2013. Similar provisions have been adopted everywhere; in the United States, it is the Volcker Rule.

aggressive price, i.e. a narrow spread, than if they had asked an institution trading stock in this company.

- Just like a dealer who can push up the price of a vehicle because they have a customer looking for that exact model, market makers can adjust their price according to their inventory or the previously communicated interests of some of their clients.

- A market maker can display a two-way (purchase and sale) or a one-way price. Equally, the quantities on offer may be different on either side. Just like for an order book, the difference between the purchase price and the sale price is called the spread and reflects the maximum possible margin (we will come back to this point).

In practice, market making can take two forms: manual, a response to a client's request for a price (by telephone or electronically); or automatic, typically added to an exchange's order book. In this second case, the exchange produces statistics showing the market shares of each participant. Market makers must quote a minimum size and a maximum spread for *each request,* or continuously. They are a liquidity provider, as distinct from the typical car dealer who is under no obligation to purchase the second-hand vehicle you have brought in[91].

Information asymmetry is a structural component of market making and is subject to particularly sustained regulatory efforts. If we go back to our car analogy, suppose the vehicle you have for sale is recalled for an engine replacement due to a manufacturing defect for which the manufacturer assumes full responsibility. Naturally, the dealer is aware of this and knows that they can make a quick buck by acquiring your car and selling it on with a new engine, without spending a penny. If you do not have access to that information – and how could you? – you will accept a lower price than you could have got. Similarly, the dealer may know (and keep hidden) that the second-hand car you want to buy is likely to require extensive repairs in the near future. What might seem like a bargain could quickly become a money pit. The same is true on a trading floor: any trader is likely to have

---

[91] Even though the industry itself understands the value of an active second-hand market, and even though margins and commissions on second-hand vehicles may be higher than on new cars.

information that their clients do not; it is their job, after all. They are required by regulation to share this information with their clients when it is relevant. Granted it is in their commercial interest to show they are better than their competitors, but it is also a regulatory and ethical obligation to put the client's interest first. Remember that a well-informed client has no reciprocal obligation to share information with the trader, who nevertheless is obliged to display a price.

The market maker's profit margin is necessarily smaller than their spread. If by chance the buyer and seller engage the market maker for execution at the same time, the market maker collects the spread without doing anything. If the market price stays the same, that is the most that can be earned. Of course, the profit or loss may increase if the market moves. Take for example a trader on company ABC who displays \$99.5/\$100 for 100 shares on each side. If two-way execution takes place, the trader will have gained (\$100 - \$99.5) x 100 = \$50. If, after asking for a quote, the client only sells 100 shares at \$99.5, the trader is left with 100 shares in position. Quite naturally, and all other things being equal, they will display \$99/\$100 to the next customer in order to reduce their average purchase price (assuming a maximum spread of \$1). If they buy again, they will be in possession of 200 shares acquired at \$99.25 on average. Their next market could be \$98.5/\$99.5. They will tend to adjust their prices according to their inventory, even if ABC does not move. If ABC now falls – because another participant displays a lower spread or bad news has just broken – our trader could find themselves making a \$97/\$98 market, which would mean a loss (albeit unrealised until the position is closed out) on the 200 shares they already own.

It is clear from this example that the trader bears a liquidity risk – the possibility of being solicited by several clients on the same side in sequence – and a market risk – the possibility that the share price changes even without a client coming to buy or sell. The spread is the margin that market makers require in return for the risks they take. Depending on their sales policy and individual risk appetite, competing traders may therefore choose to quote different spreads.

4. Why it matters

We do not need to look too far back in the history books to find the answer: the 2008 crisis drove proprietary trading away from large financial institutions in favour of a market-making obligation enshrined in law. The French regulator (for example) does not take this obligation lightly: failure to comply may result in criminal prosecution, regardless of any sanctions that the employer may impose.

Whether these measures are proving effective for overall financial stability is still a matter for debate. Of course, the remodelling of certain remuneration structures that rewarded risk-taking and the removal of proprietary trading have helped make the financial system safer at a macroeconomic level. But at what cost? First, the jobs cost, with market finance overstaffed and shrinking since 2008, not unlike the automotive industry in the 1980s and 1990s. Staff reductions concern all categories of personnel – traders, salespeople, IT specialists, back-office operators, etc. – and have not run their course. Second, the even greater impact on the cost of risk. Faced with a demand that is rising slowly but surely commensurate with the size of global savings, the supply of risk management is decreasing significantly, with a number of participants having seen their absorption capacity reduced by their management, supervisory bodies or both. Incurring risk requires a reward. If this reward is under such pressure that it gradually disappears, what additional marginal cost is there for end investors? No one knows. You might think that the sky-high profits reported by major international banks are still obscene. This is not the case: the weighted average cost of capital of international financial institutions is estimated at 10% over the long term. Most are well below this level since the crisis, which is now a decade old. The conclusion is irrefutable: they destroy value[92].

---

[92] The McKinsey consulting firm estimates that the major banks' return on equity from their capital market activities was slashed after the crisis because of regulatory changes, going from 20% to 7%. See "Global Corporate and Investment Banking: An Agenda for Change", September 2011.

Make no mistake, the end investors here are you and me. Whether it's through pension funds, mutual funds or life insurance policies, each individual *ultimately* bears the risk that their savings will depreciate, and it is precisely this risk against which they would like to (at least partially) protect themselves.

XIII. Financing and refinancing

1. What are we talking about?

The main characteristic of a bank is having access to the national and/or international money markets – so it can fulfil its remit of creating money through credit. Ultimately, a bank is just a series of *receivables* on the assets side against a series of *payables* on the liabilities side. In other words, it is a mutual series of promises to pay and receive.

Access to money markets means that a bank can continually borrow very large amounts of money. This is possible because its creditors can be reasonably certain at any given moment that they will be repaid when the time comes. Liabilities are used to finance assets, and the difference in remuneration – interest received on loans minus interest paid on debt – generates a big share of revenues.

When a bank is created, its balance sheet is like that of any other company:

Assets		Liabilities	
$100,000	Cash and cash equivalents		
		Shareholders' equity	$100,000

Shareholders' equity is contributed by the shareholders who own the capital and therefore the company. If this bank lends $100,000 to an individual for the purchase of an apartment, a receivable appears directly under assets. The bank actually pays out $100,000 into the account of the borrower, which is then paid to the seller of the apartment on the day of the sale:

Assets		Liabilities	
$100,000	Cash and cash equivalents		
$100,000	*Loan*		
		Debt	*$100,000*
		Shareholders' equity	$100,000

To ensure its balance sheet remains balanced, the bank must borrow $100,000 and record the debt under liabilities. If you were paying attention during the chapter on interest rates, you will know what happens next: if the loan has a maturity of 20 years, the bank can also finance itself over 20 years, or for a shorter period, which will increase its margin (remember the term structure of interest rates). An operation in which assets and liabilities do not have the same maturity is called *transformation*; financial institutions exploit this principle massively to manufacture margins.

The more loans, the bigger the balance sheet. If the bank lends $10,000,000 to its customers, its debts increase by the same amount:

Assets		Liabilities	
$100,000	Cash and cash equivalents		
$10,000,000	Loans		
		Debt	$10,000,000
		Shareholders' equity	$100,000

In reality, part of this debt consists of customer deposits in current accounts:

Assets		Liabilities	
$100,000	Cash and cash equivalents		
$10,000,000	Loans		
		Deposits	$2,000,000
		Debt	$8,000,000
		Shareholders' equity	$100,000

This bank's leverage is ($10,100,000/$100,000) = 101. Alternatively, the capital ratio is 0.99% (= $100,000/$10,100,000). Leverage (or capital ratio) is a measure of the size of the bank's balance sheet relative to its capital. Take the example of a deposit on a property purchase. Even though the price is the same, two individuals offering different deposits present a different risk. Similarly, if two banks have a similar-sized balance sheet, the one with the most equity is stronger in theory.

To fully understand the issue of leverage, let us assume that a deterioration in the economic environment results in 2% of borrowers being unable to repay their loan. The bank is forced to record a loss in its receivables portfolio, which must be written down by $200,000 (= 2% of total receivables of $10,000,000). It is of course equally unthinkable to tell customers that their deposits will be eroded or creditors that they will not get back all of the $8,000,000 they have lent. The balance sheet now looks like this:

Assets		Liabilities	
$100,000	Cash and cash equivalents		
$9,800,000	Loans		
		Deposits	$2,000,000
		Debt	$8,000,000
		Shareholders' equity	-$100,000

No company can have negative equity, because this would imply that its shareholders have an obligation to inject another $100,000 of capital. Limited liability in commercial law requires that the shareholders' liability be strictly limited to the amount of their contribution, nothing more. A financial institution or any limited-liability company with negative equity is therefore bankrupt.

In the example above, with $100,000 of equity and $10,000,000 of loans, it is clear that any situation leading to more than 1% of doubtful receivables will almost immediately bring about the bank's bankruptcy. You may say that assets could be seized and sold to replenish capital. Sure, that is a possibility, but the obligation incumbent upon all companies to keep their balance sheet balanced means that bankruptcy could be recognised well before the real estate assets are liquidated, even in a favourable market. Especially if the economic climate deteriorates to the point of forcing certain borrowers to interrupt their repayments, you can easily see how difficult and time-consuming it might be to sell off assets, whatever their quality.

This long introduction has hopefully reinforced two concepts:
- a bank's liabilities are used to finance its assets, i.e. essentially its credit activity,
- this activity inevitably swells the balance sheet and therefore increases leverage, although this cannot rise indefinitely without jeopardising the solvency (and therefore the very existence) of the bank.

Armed with this knowledge, you can see how managing the balance sheet of a financial institution is an existential exercise:
- The size of the balance sheet indicates the magnitude of the risks carried. After all, a bank whose customers all honour their debt can never go into default, but the more customers it has, the more likely it is that some will default.
- While each loan generates income, the more a bank lends, the more profitable it is. This is a powerful incentive to increase the leverage ratio. Banks are expected to finance the economy. They can do so only by taking risks and having a big enough balance sheet.

- The size of the assets determines the size of the liabilities, i.e. the amount of debt that the bank must incur to support its activity. Not surprisingly, the stock of debt must be carefully managed: it is much easier to find a client seeking a mortgage than a creditor[93] willing to lend, even to a large, well-established institution. Moreover, the more a bank borrows, the more it has to pay to convince creditors to bear its risk[94].

In reality, banks are limited by their own funds, i.e. the amount of capital at their disposal as a cushion. The size of the balance sheet has an absolute ceiling, established by regulatory texts.[95] What happens when this ceiling is reached or is close to being reached? Generally speaking, how does a bank control the size of its balance sheet?

If receivables are clogging the balance sheet, preventing it from expanding and *ultimately* causing an increase in the cost of borrowing (therefore squeezing the bank's margins), there is a simple solution: get rid of certain receivables, preferably the riskiest or least profitable. This is, of course, easier said than done. The same desire exists in industry, and the corresponding service is called *factoring*. A service provider takes on a company's receivables and in turn lends the same amount to said company. When the customers pay their invoices, the service provider is reimbursed through these payments.

Unfortunately, this service requires the ability to lend money and therefore a banking license, so not surprisingly it is offered by banks or subsidiaries of banking groups. Who can provide the equivalent service in the banking world? Widespread factoring would essentially lead to banks passing on receivables to one another without really addressing the fundamental issue

---

[93] I use the term creditor in both senses: the bank has a receivable with the individual who takes out a mortgage, and it borrows from its own creditors to balance its accounts.

[94] There is an optimum level; finding and maintaining it is the objective of a bank's asset-liability management.

[95] The Basel Committee, which is part of the Bank for International Settlements, has set a maximum leverage ratio of 25x. However, the calculation is not as simple as the one we performed earlier because some balance sheet items require special treatment.

of reducing balance sheet receivables across the *entire banking system* in absolute terms.

The solution is to securitise receivables. In the case of real estate loans, a securitisation transaction involves taking a large number of loans and transferring them to an ad hoc company, which issues shares and bonds that are sold to end investors – pension funds, insurers, etc. The bank sells its receivables to the company, which enables it to recover cash and balance sheet capacity.

2.   The trading floor

On a trading floor, traders buy and sell shares to manage their portfolio, including derivatives. These portfolios consume cash to the extent that securities purchased[96] require settlement/delivery. As a result, a trading floor needs significant cash flows to function normally. The ability to mobilise cash cheaply is a major competitive advantage.

Assets held are usually extremely liquid, so they are relatively easy to lend and borrow. It is tempting for an operator to *refinance* them to benefit from leverage. Suppose a trader has a liquidity reserve of $100 million to finance their activity. Once they reach this limit by purchasing cash products, they are blocked and can manage only their existing positions.

That is, unless they *refinance* these positions. If they find a counterpart willing to take certain assets as collateral for cash, they can free up resources and increase their outstanding assets. And there is, in theory, no limit to how often they can do this. In practice, of course, such a scenario is prevented by the regulatory maximum leverage. Nevertheless, in reality, an opportunity

---

[96] Remember from Chapter 7 "Cash and derivatives" that equities are cash products, so they must be settled in full. See Chapter 15 "Delta management" for more on delta and hedging. Only cash products consume significant amounts of cash. Derivatives are subject only to initial margins and daily margin calls.

to refinance increases the size of a portfolio, thus creating leverage, controlling liquidity and expanding the balance sheet[97].

3.   Central bank intervention

The primary function of a central bank is to act as a lender of last resort. This means that, in a dislocated money market, where people might be looking at one another with suspicion and no one wants to lend, the central bank is the only one that can intervene to inject liquidity[98] because it can create this liquidity in unlimited quantities.

However, when such an intervention takes place, central banks do not just lend anything to anyone; economic agents must meet certain conditions:

- They must have a specific financial institution status and therefore accept the supervision of the national financial authorities that regulate them;
- They must hold assets eligible for central bank financing.

Indeed, a central bank never lends without collateral. It engages only in refinancing, not financing. All cash loans are secured by an asset or a group of assets determined by the central bank according to what is needed at that time and the objective it has set itself. For example, a French sovereign bond issued by the French Treasury is naturally eligible for refinancing by the Banque de France (BdF) and the European Central Bank (ECB). However, certain securities such as those issued in securitisation operations may not be eligible depending on the central bank's objective at a given point in time.

---

[97] The fundamental difference between securitisation and refinancing is that in a securitisation transaction, the assets and/or receivables are permanently transferred to one or more third parties. In the case of refinancing, the transfer of ownership is temporary.

[98] It is also responsible for setting the price at which this liquidity is injected.

4. Why it matters

I included this chapter primarily because today's interbank money markets operate mainly on a collateralised finance, or refinancing, logic. An economic agent that has acquired a receivable or asset temporarily or permanently assigns this receivable or asset in return for a cash payment that will be repaid with interest. The amounts involved are colossal, especially since central banks in the United States, Japan and Europe have assiduously pursued a policy of "quantitative easing", meaning they have massively refinanced sovereign bonds – and sometimes other types of receivables such as securitisation units.

Moreover, away from money markets, refinancing is a trading room's fundamental mechanism for controlling its current cash consumption, leverage and balance sheet footprint. As such, most major institutions have established extremely active refinancing activities, often categorised by the nature of the underlying asset (equities, sovereign bonds, corporate bonds, etc.).

XIV. Optionality

1. What are we talking about?

An option is a derivative product that gives its holder the right, but not the obligation, to carry out a transaction. Whereas a forward contract obliges the parties to trade, option holders may decide not to do anything at maturity.

Take our wheat example in Chapter 5 on deferred delivery. As we saw, being able to deliver at a future date introduces many issues into a market that would otherwise ultimately be quite simple. Let's suppose that spot wheat is trading at $100 per tonne and three-month forward wheat at $110. If someone buys a tonne of wheat forward, they must take delivery in three months and pay $110. If they refuse, they will be considered in default.

Now let's suppose that they enter into a contract that gives them the right, but not the obligation, to buy the wheat at $110 in three months' time. Of course, if they exercise this right, they will have to pay $110 and take delivery of the wheat, just as if they had subscribed to a deferred delivery. But now they have the option to change their mind without being considered in default. Why might they decline to exercise their option? Well, perhaps they no longer need the wheat because they have sufficient stocks, for example if they are an industrial buyer or the expected demand has not materialised. Or maybe they are a speculator and realise there is no money to be made. Even if the purchase is still justified, they will not exercise the option if they can buy spot wheat for less. If, for example, spot wheat costs $104 per tonne when the option expires, it makes more sense to buy the spot wheat. If it costs $120, however, exercising the option and selling the wheat on immediately will bring about a tidy profit.

As we can see, the decision to exercise this option depends on various factors, primarily the price on expiry. But the most important question is how much should the buyer pay for the *opportunity* to do nothing at all? It is fairly apparent that this is a kind of insurance. The buyer has guaranteed themselves a maximum price of $110 while keeping the possibility of paying less. They can't expect to get that privilege for free.

Intuitively, the option price depends on the following parameters at least:

- The spot price of wheat today, which we will call S. The more S increases, the more the option has value: if C is its price, C is an increasing function of S;

- The interest rate (which we will call r): if the buyer keeps their capital until the option expires, they will get interest on it. C is an increasing function of the r;

- The strike price, $110 in this case. Evidently, it makes more sense to buy a tonne of wheat at $110 than at $120. We will call this price K. C is a decreasing function of K (the more K increases, the more C decreases);

- C depends on the price of storage, insurance and safekeeping. The buyer saves money by not paying the spot price, but the seller must maintain a stock and reflect these costs, at least partly, in C. C is an increasing function of P, the carrying cost;

- An insurance that only really features when there is risk. This is harder to understand, but bear with me. If the price of wheat has varied between $98 and $103 per tonne over the last 15 years, it is reasonable to assume that the option to buy it at $110 hedges an upside risk that does not really exist. So the final fundamental parameter is the variability of S over the period between now and when the option expires. This is known as the standard deviation, or volatility, of S[99], and is denoted by σ.

In summary:

$$C = f(S, r, K, P, \sigma)$$

The parameters also depend on the underlying. For example, P in the case of wheat represents the cost of carrying one tonne of wheat. In the case of a share, it would be equal to the dividend: the purchaser of the option is not the bearer of the share and therefore receives no dividend, so this must be taken into account. Having said that, the above formula is extremely generic,

---

[99] Or more precisely the standard deviation of the time series of daily S yields.

even if specific adaptations must be made when calculating the parameters[100].

Suppose the option is worth $1.5 in our example. Today, the buyer pays $1.5, and this is called the option *premium*. Three months later, the option is worthless if S is $105. Who would pay $110 when they can pay $105 for the same thing[101]? In this case, we say that the option has expired *out of the money*. However, if S = $120, the option is worth $10, i.e. the difference between S and K (the strike price of $110). This difference is the intrinsic value, and the option is said to expire *in the money*. So the buyer will in fact have paid $110 for the wheat and $1.5 for the option, so a total of $111.5 – still less than $120.

Our example focuses on an option to buy (call option), but of course there are options to sell, known as put options. So now, the operation is reversed: the buyer of the put option has the right, but not the obligation, to sell the wheat at maturity. If S = $120, they will not exercise the option because the put is out of the money. If S = $95, the intrinsic value of the put option is $15 (= $110 - $95) and the option holder will exercise it. They will have sold their wheat for $95 - $1.5 = $93.5 since they have to subtract the option premium.

I could write several chapters on options, and there is plenty of literature out there for all degrees of expertise, from someone with a PhD in statistics to a casual trader just setting out. Dozens of different option types have emerged, varying according to the characteristics of the reference price, the period over which the option can be exercised, the activation or deactivation of the option based on S (knock-in or knock-out), etc. It is outside the scope of this book to focus on the technical aspect of options, but we will explore two simple characteristics that make them extremely powerful instruments: asymmetry and convexity.

---

[100] In the case of a currency, the carrying cost is the interest rate, which is already present elsewhere, so P = 0.

[101] This is where we can see the need for fungibility: all this reasoning holds only if the buyer is assured of having wheat of identical quality, whether that be today at spot price, forward in three months, or spot in three months.

2.   Asymmetry

Suppose you bought a wheat forward contract one month ago at $100 per tonne. The contract expires in a few minutes and you are keen to find out if you are in the money. To keep things simple, let's assume you are a speculator, so you are not involved in storing or producing the wheat.

The contract obliges you to take delivery of the tonne of wheat that is offered to you at $100. Since you have neither a use for it nor the experience to store it, you have no choice but to sell this wheat on. If the spot wheat price is $105 per tonne, you immediately make a $5 profit. Ker-ching! If it is $95, nice try, but you're $5 out of pocket. Figure 14.1 shows the payoff of the position, i.e. the profit or loss *at maturity* based on the spot price of the underlying.

Figure 14.1 - *Payoff of a forward contract*

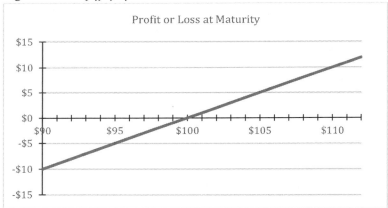

What about an option? Suppose that instead of entering into a forward contract you purchased a call option with a strike price of $100 and a premium of $3:

- If the underlying ends up at $105, happy days: you exercise the option to buy the wheat at $100, and then sell it at $105. Your profit is $5, minus the initial premium of $3.
- If the underlying ends up at $95, you let the option expire without exercising it. You lose $3, i.e. the premium.

This payoff is represented in Figure 14.2[102] (the buyer of a forward contract in blue, the buyer of an option in red).

Figure 14.2 - *Payoff of a call option*

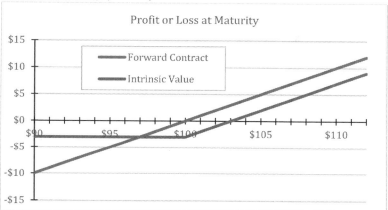

The payoff is no longer linear or symmetrical. If the price of wheat drops to $90 per tonne, the holder of a forward contract loses $10, while the option holder loses only $3. An option thus creates an asymmetry that protects the holder from a potentially very large loss. Exactly the same applies for a put option, as shown in Figure 14.3 (the seller of a forward contract in blue, the buyer of a put option in red).

---

[102] Its exact formula is max (S - K, 0) – P, where K = strike price, S = spot price of the underlying, P = option premium. We are neglecting that the option premium was paid upfront; strictly speaking, it would have to be capitalised at the risk-free rate.

Figure 14.3. - *Payoff of a put option*

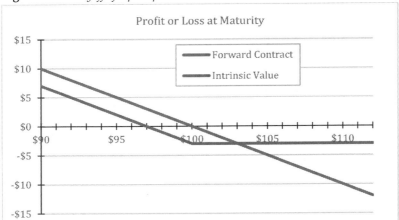

An option therefore has insurance value: buyers pay a premium, and in return their losses are limited. No wonder optionality has proved so popular, it now being possible to calculate an exact price for almost any combination (option and underlying). We will dig a little deeper on this later.

3.   Convexity

Payoff is a measure of profitability at expiry, i.e. when the derivative matures. What about before the option matures? To answer this question, which is actually the most difficult, we need to consider the option's intrinsic value, i.e. the difference between S (spot price) and K (strike price) at any given moment. Suppose someone offers a call option for less than its intrinsic value. If you buy it, you can make a definite profit.

Say that K = $100, S = $110 and P = $3. Once again, S is the spot price of wheat today and P the option premium. The intrinsic value of the option is S - K = $10. So you buy the option for $3 and sell wheat forward at 110 $ (to keep things simple, let's assume that the forward price of wheat is equal to the spot price). You exercise the option on maturity, so you have a tonne of wheat delivered for an outlay of $100. Under the terms of the forward contract, you must sell it on at $110, giving you a profit of $10. Taking away the premium of $3 leaves you with a net gain of $7, whatever the price of wheat at maturity.

Simply put, a call option is never worth less than its intrinsic value, otherwise buyers would have the chance of a risk-free gain[103]. The same applies, of course, to a put option. Since an option always expires at its intrinsic value, if you bought it for less, you made a very good deal. But the same applies during the life of the option, meaning that the difference between its market price – available for example from a market maker – and its intrinsic value is always positive, and this is called the *time value*. It is the market value of the protection that the option offers its holder. The farther you are from expiry, the more useful the insurance is and the higher the time value. Figure 14.4 shows the market value of the option before its maturity (in red).

Figure 14.4 - *Market value of a call option before maturity*

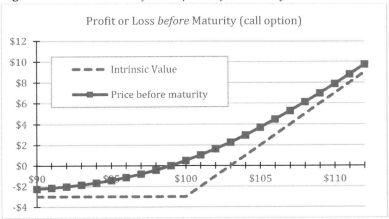

This is actually the mark-to-market of the option. The red curve is above the blue line, and the difference between the two represents the time value. This graph illustrates what is called the *convexity* of an option. Its price is not linear, unlike the intrinsic value (dotted blue). The curve is convex, i.e. when the price of the underlying varies by $1, the option price does not always vary by the same amount. When S is around $90, the red curve is almost

---

[103] Therefore a definite loss for the person who sells it. A derivative is always a zero-sum contract.

horizontal: the price of the option varies very little as a function of S. This makes sense since there is little use having the right to buy wheat at $100 when you can immediately get your hands on it for around $90. Conversely, when S is around $110, the price of the option varies almost as much as S. Again, perfectly logical, but this time for the opposite reason: having the right to buy at $100 something worth $105 has a lot of value, and this value increases with S.

Contrast this with the price of a forward contract, which is proportional to that of the underlying. Just take a look back at Figures 14.2 and 14.3. For every $1 change in S, the blue line also changes by $1.

4.   Calculating the price of an option

The principle of an option has existed in all walks of life for a long time. The American consumer market institutionalised this notion with its famous "30-day money back guarantee", i.e. the promise of an unconditional refund for 30 days if you are not satisfied with the product. There are myriad other examples. In French commercial law, the buyer of a property can pull out up to seven days after signing the sale agreement. Similarly, the buyer is generally protected by a clause specifying that the deal is subject to a loan being agreed. As any seller will tell you, this clause is annoying because it essentially takes the property off the market for a few months. All this should have convinced you that every option has a value. It may not be possible to monetise it, but it does exist. In most property purchases, the right to purchase cannot be transferred to a third party if the original buyer is unable to secure a loan. If this were the case, the defaulting buyer could potentially assign the agreement to another buyer who is interested in the property and in a position to buy it for cash. The option is real, but impossible to monetise – its sole purpose is to help the buyer recover their 10% deposit should they fail to secure financing.

The same applies to financial products. The notion of optionality had existed for a while, but the problem of valuation persisted until 1973, when two mathematicians, Fischer Black and Myron Scholes, proposed a closed formula – i.e. exact and easily calculable – for valuing a share option[104]. This was an extraordinary result, insofar as it finally offered the possibility of calculating the price of an option without making an assumption about the expected return of the underlying – an assumption that had blocked any progress until then. Black and Scholes' USP was *delta-hedging*: they came to the conclusion that the return of a delta-hedged portfolio can only be the risk-free return, i.e. the risk-free rate[105]. This remarkable breakthrough earned Scholes (Black had since died) the Nobel Prize in Economics in 1997 and changed the options market forever. Armed with this formula, participants went wild. Volumes exploded, and the creativity of financial engineers led them very quickly to even more complex derivative products known as "structured products", which would be sold *en masse* to all kinds of clients.

If you would like to know more, there is plenty of literature out there on the Black-Scholes formula, as well as on its (now widely known) weaknesses. One of these is its assumption that underlying prices follow a Brownian motion, i.e. a particular form of random movement. As we have said before, the truth is rarely so straightforward. The prices of financial products *do not follow* a Brownian motion, which totally invalidates the Black-Scholes formula. Many other models have emerged, but since at the end of the day no one knows the laws that govern financial asset prices, any modelling exercise is broadly doomed to failure.

Specifically, the problem is not that the price is wrong. As a first approximation, it is possible to find models that produce prices in line with what can be observed on the markets[106]. Their great weakness is actually their robustness and sensitivity. During a shock, especially a downward

---

[104] A European option on a non-dividend-paying stock. See "The Pricing of Options and Corporate Liabilities", Fischer Black & Myron Scholes, *Journal of Political Economy*, Vol. 81, May-June 1973.

[105] See Chapter 15 "Delta management" for an explanation of portfolio delta.

[106] Observing the price of a product on a market, while being necessary for mark-to-market valuation, does not immediately validate a new model. If most of the participants base themselves on Black-Scholes, a Black-Scholes price will be observed. A new model will be obliged to stick to the prices of the old one, i.e. to reproduce Black-Scholes prices even if they are held to be false.

shock, no one knows how the price of a share, or its volatility (which is a crucial component of the Black-Scholes model), will evolve.

It is therefore in capturing market variations that these models are unreliable: whereas a trader might justifiably feel that a portfolio is valued and hedged correctly, they don't really know. In reality, the model will break down immediately when confronted with a real shock. For small market movements, everything will be fine. Initially, the portfolio will distort as the model predicted. Outside of these perfect yet unrealistic conditions, nothing works anymore, and the situation deteriorates during violent crises. We've seen that markets have a bad habit of being leptokurtic. The analogy that springs to mind is rogue waves. These absolutely incredible waves were thought for decades to be nothing more than a myth. Dozens of feet tall, they appear out of nowhere and have left countless wrecks in their wake; generations of ships were simply not built to cope with them. The same is true of rogue waves on the ocean of capital markets. We now know that they exist, but nobody can predict when they are going to appear, and because no one is prepared the damage is incredibly severe.

5. Why it matters

Before considering the value that options have brought to the general workings of financial markets, let's think for a moment about wheat producers. How do they manage their harvest over time? How can they protect themselves against, or on the contrary benefit from, a price variation? How do they plan their investments in machinery, grain and labour? What information do they have at any given moment?

Derivatives are not just speculation; they are primarily used to manage risks, i.e. to enable economic agents to optimise their risk/reward profile and trade at the *right price*. Some actors will want to bear certain risks, others will not. The notion of optionality introduces previously unavailable choices, in particular through asymmetry, which creates a guarantee equivalent to insurance. The added value of Black-Scholes and the starting point of a major paradigm shift can above all be found in the number of concrete applications. For the first time, it became possible to create a liquid insurance market on wheat, oil, currencies, shares, bonds and interest rates, and later credit, electricity, climate, etc. Speculation has naturally become a dominant factor, particularly because the market has understandably taken a long time to become efficient. It is one thing to know that the price of a call depends on the volatility of its underlying, but what value of the volatility makes sense? The one that's been observed recently? The one that's anticipated in the near future? It took time for stakeholders to converge on an answer and to refine their understanding of what really needed to be added to the wonderful formula that had been presented to them. But there is a *vast natural market* between insurance buyers and sellers willing to be remunerated for their risks. Speculators only appeared afterwards.

Black & Scholes, and more generally the mastery of the optional payoff, had an additional effect: they opened the door to a new field of investigation, a "new frontier". The financial engineers of the late 1980s kept following in the footsteps of their elders. Stochastic calculus, i.e. the mathematics of random phenomena, has made tremendous progress and new payoffs have emerged[107]. The reward for each innovation was immediate: a bank capable of offering a unique payoff was guaranteed exclusivity for as long as it took its competitors to catch up.

Have end investors benefited from these conceptual advances? Unquestionably. The big investment banks didn't create payoffs for kicks. They were immediately distributed to pension funds, insurers and individuals of varying wealth. Demand was there: the massive drop in interest rates over the past 25 years has led to a hunt for yield and performance from all investors, especially money managers concerned with delivering concrete results to their clients. It is in this context of growing demand that the supply was born, and new products appeared with innovative and sometimes surprising characteristics.

This golden age lasted until 2007-2008[108] and the near bankruptcy of Bear Stearns, leading to its takeover by JP Morgan. The crisis did not emerge from

---

[107] American, Bermudan, barrier, ratchet, lookback, digital and compound options, among many others.

[108] While there were ups and downs, previous crises had not diminished the banks' ability to accept and recycle risk. Lehman's bankruptcy changed everything because it froze money markets and consequently damaged the banks' ability to refinance.

derivatives on one asset class or another, but from *cash* real estate, like most previous banking crises. It is true that the very high level of leverage in the banking industry, and the chronic inability of risk models to measure randomness, have precipitated the outcome[109] .

So, quite simply, it matters because quantitative mastery of optionality has been the major financial innovation of the last 50 years.

Regardless of whether it is profitable, a bank that cannot refinance is immediately in trouble, if not bankrupt.

[109] Mortgage securitisation – which is nothing more than a real estate credit derivative – has significantly worsened the situation. Pricing and risk models, particularly those of rating agencies, have proven wholly inadequate to predict randomness. See "S&P Ends Legal Woes Paying $1.5 Billion Fine to U.S., States" Bloomberg.com, 3 Feb. 2015, or "Moody's to Pay $864 Million to Settle Inquiry Into Inflated Ratings", New York Times, 13 Jan. 2017

XV.   Delta hedging

1.   What are we talking about?

Let's say a portfolio contains a quantity Q_S of an underlying S, and Q_D of a derivative D on the same underlying S. The first thing to look at is the value of this portfolio at a given time t, which means pricing each of the instruments held as correctly as possible. So let's call π the corresponding value of the portfolio, which is written thus:

$$\Pi(\dots, S, t, \dots) = Q_D \times D(\dots, S, t, \dots) + Q_S \times S(t)$$

where: D(..., S,t,...) is the price of the derivative and S the price of the underlying. The parenthesis (..., S,t,...) indicates that D depends on a number of parameters that feature the value of the underlying S and the date t. In the case of a forward contract, D would also depend on the interest rate until maturity, storage and insurance costs for a physical commodity, or its yield for a share, a bond or any other financial asset. Similarly, if the derivative is an option, the strike price and volatility must be added at the very least. But S on the other hand depends only on time.

Once this formula has been applied, it becomes possible to calculate the value of the portfolio at any time. But what is the risk? As discussed earlier, measuring risk is the same as looking at the variability of parameters. The first source of uncertainty is obviously S. If S is a random variable like any time series that describes the price of an instrument set by an efficient market of buyers and sellers, no one can know what S will be worth even in a few seconds' time, regardless of the value observed at t. Any investor would therefore want to measure the change in their wealth as a function of S, if possible before a change occurs, so that they could adjust their portfolio – i.e. change Q_D and Q_S – if needed.

Mathematics provides a relatively simple tool to answer this question, a tool that does not require any particular assumption about S, D or their movements. Just as well, because the movements of S are random and unpredictable, and those of D depend on S. This tool is a *limited Taylor expansion* and is expressed as follows:

$$f(x_0 + h) - f(x_0) \approx h \times \Delta$$

If a function f(.) is known at a point x_0, it is possible to estimate the value of this function near x_0. When we are close to x_0, at a distance h, the difference between the two values of the function $f(x_0 + h)$ and $f(x_0)$ is proportional to h. The coefficient of proportionality, Δ in this case, is the first derivative of f in x_0 : $\Delta = f'(x_0)$, i.e. in practice, a value that is fairly easy to calculate when f is known [110].

All this has already been mentioned in Chapter 8 on risk management, but let's go a little further and do a limited Taylor expansion of π given a small variation of S:

$$\Pi(S + h, t) = Q_D \times D(S + h, t) + Q_S \times [S(t) + h]$$

From the above, we have:

$$D(S + h, t) = D(S, t) + h \times \Delta$$

where: $\Delta = D'(S)$ is the first derivative of D in S.

After a few manipulations, we eventually end up with:

$$\Pi(S + h, t) - \Pi(S, t) = [Q_D \times \Delta + Q_S] \times h$$

What happens if $Q_D \times \Delta + Q_S = 0$? It follows that $\pi (S + h, t) = \pi (S, t)$, i.e. the portfolio does not change in value. This is quite remarkable because in this case whatever the price variation of the underlying – materialised by h – the investor does not lose or gain money. Managing the delta of a portfolio

---

[110] The most general formula for limited Taylor expansion is:

$$f(x_0 + h) = f(x_0) + \frac{1}{1!}h.f'(x_0) + \frac{1}{2!}.h^2.f''(x_0) + \frac{1}{3!}.h^3.f'''(x_0) + \cdots + \frac{1}{n!}.h^n.f^{(n)}(x_0) + \cdots$$

and involves f(.) derivatives of higher orders. The only assumptions are: f(.) is derivable n times, and h << S, i.e. h is "small compared with" S. In our example, these assumptions are easily verified.

means exactly this: *adjusting its composition so that its value does not change when the price of the underlying varies.* A portfolio built this way is "delta hedged" if:

$$Q_S = -Q_D \times \Delta$$

i.e. the quantity of the underlying depends on the quantity of the derivative and its delta.

A few things need clarifying:
- One of our assumptions is that h is small compared with S. In other words, this only works for small variations, typically a few percent either way. Limited Taylor expansion does not necessarily hold for larger fluctuations, particularly a market surge or crash; it is an approximation after all.
- In practice, the delta must be adjusted regularly. The more frequently this happens, the more immune the portfolio is to market movements, but because of the transaction costs on S and D, this solution may not be financially viable. Conversely, infrequent coverage may not be expensive to implement, but the protective effect is weakened in a market that is likely to change rapidly. In practice, professionals hedge at least once a day, and much more often in volatile markets.
- What is valid for a single asset and its derivative can easily be extended to much larger and more diversified portfolios[111].
- Remember that the only specific assumption we have made is that h is small compared with S, and that derivatives have a price computed from a mathematically derivable function. In practice, this is always the case.[112] If we were talking about interest rates,

---

[111] Unless the portfolio contains derivatives whose price depends on several underlyings, in which case it is also necessary to consider how the various assets depend on one another, i.e. their correlation. Given that it is impossible to predict the variation of a single underlying over time, predicting the correlation of several is unsurprisingly a bit of a minefield.

[112] For obvious reasons related to risk management 101: no trader would be allowed to trade a product whose price they can only observe, without being able to model it. Indeed, observing a price does not give any indication as to its mathematical derivability, and therefore whether it can be delta hedged.

corn or electricity, the principle would therefore be the same: calculate the portfolio's Δ on the underlying in question, determine the acceptable risk and adjust the portfolio accordingly by buying/selling S or D.

- In real life, it is very often easier and cheaper to trade S than D to adapt the portfolio.

2. What's the point of all this?

In an earlier chapter, we looked at the role and the main characteristics of a market maker, and the regulation imposed on banks – particularly in France – to intervene only as market makers.

Suppose a client calls a trader to buy or sell a derivative, for example an option on an index, a share, a bond, a currency, an interest rate, oil, whatever. The client's motives are what they are. Whether they want to speculate or protect themselves from a future risk must have no impact on the trader's decision to make a price, on the short- and long-term risk they accept or on their ability to guarantee a margin on that price. Put differently, if the client takes a position, traders in theory are not obliged to take the opposite position (i.e. risk) because derivatives are a zero-sum game.

Delta management solves this problem: the market maker can make a price (incorporating a margin) on the product that the client wishes to trade, and if the client actually decides to trade, the trader has a mathematically robust methodology protecting against market movements[113].

The client therefore ends up carrying the product they have bought or sold, and they can delta hedge the risks if they so desire. But the risk transferred to the bank will *automatically* be covered by the market maker, who will therefore be able to materialise and retain their margin. The money earned

---

[113] Note that portfolio management protects only against market movements. The creditworthiness of the client and operational risks (such as an ill-timed IT failure) are risks that the trader must assess to determine the aggressiveness of the price he is making – if he even wants to trade this product with this client.

by the trader on a transaction of this type remunerates the bank's ability to *make prices*, i.e. ultimately its ability to manage portfolio risk so as to minimise losses during the life of the product, whether it is unwound with another client or brought to maturity.

Delta management therefore allows derivative risk to be transferred extremely efficiently. It is quite simply the main mechanism that allows banks – and more generally any participant – to operate as intermediaries by choosing their risks.

3.   Taking the next step

So far, we've looked at a first-order derivative, Δ. What happens when we integrate second-order derivatives? If h is not small compared with S, the first-order limited Taylor expansion of D is no longer sufficient because the second order is necessary. Another reason to go in this direction is to study the variation of Δ with S. It's one thing to have a portfolio adequately hedged, but what will become of it when the market goes up or down?

The second-order limited Taylor expansion of a function is:

$$f(x_0 + h) - f(x_0) \approx h \times \varDelta + \frac{1}{2} \times h^2 \times \varGamma$$

where *gamma* Γ is the second derivative of f(.). If we follow the reasoning set out above, we get[114]:

$$\Pi(S + h, t) = \Pi(S, t) + Q_D \times h \times \varDelta + \frac{1}{2} \times Q_D \times h^2 \times \varGamma + Q_S \times h$$

If the initial portfolio is delta hedged (or delta neutral), $Q_D \times \Delta + Q_S = 0$:

$$\Pi(S + h, t) = \Pi(S, t) + \frac{1}{2} \times Q_D \times h^2 \times \varGamma$$

------

[114] In view of:

$$D(S + h, t) = D(S, t) + h \times \varDelta + \frac{1}{2} \times h^2 \times \varGamma$$

This formula shows a change in the value of h², and not in h as is the case with the delta. The practical consequences of this result are more apparent in a graph. Figure 15.1 shows the change in the value of the portfolio Π (vertical axis) as a function of h (horizontal axis), depending on whether Δ or Γ dominates.

Figure 15.1 - *Delta and gamma (> 0)*

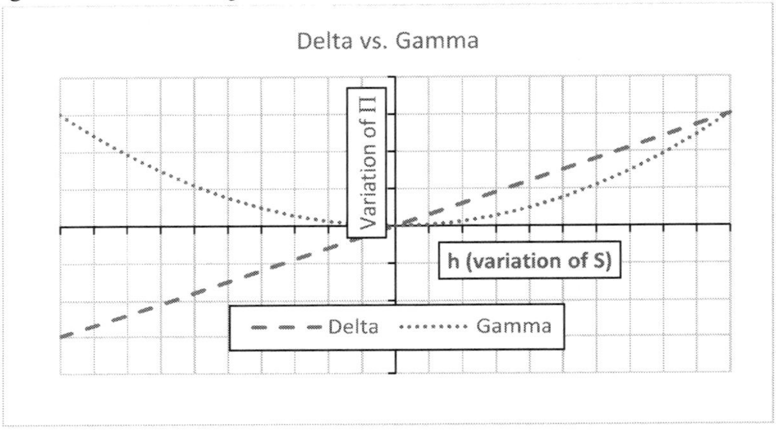

When the portfolio is not Δ neutral, its variation is written: $\Pi(S + h, t) - \Pi(S, t) = [Q_D \times \Delta + Q_S] \times h$. It is the formula of a straight line (the dashed line above). It is centred on 0, i.e. the current position value, where delta effects largely dominate gamma effects (which are second order). The two curves do not coexist (because the Γ curve here exists only if the portfolio is Δ-hedged). To improve readability, the two are not to the same scale.

In plain English:
- Close to the centre, Δ dominates and the red curve is very close to 0. Away from the centre, the opposite is true.
- Δ is asymmetric: the portfolio loses value on the left (if the market falls), whereas its value increases on the right (if the market moves upward). On the contrary, the profit or loss resulting from Γ is the same on both sides.

Of course, the opposite situation also exists (Figure 15.2).

Figure 15.2 - *Delta and Gamma (< 0)*

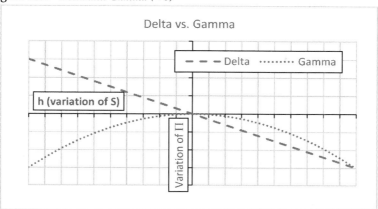

When the gamma of a portfolio is positive, the curve is oriented upwards and the portfolio is called "gamma plus (+)"; in the opposite scenario, it is called "gamma minus (–)"[115]. The same portfolio whose delta has been neutralised then reacts to any movement in either direction.

For a trader, these graphs express the following dilemma: faced with uncertainty and randomness, it is tempting to maintain a delta-neutral position, even though it may not be easy or cheap. Near the current level, the portfolio is fairly protected. But delta-neutrality creates a second-order exposure to h^2. One that could quickly become very painful (or profitable) if the market moves violently in either direction. Should you opt for a delta exposure and be exposed to a move in the wrong direction? Or perhaps you should choose a delta-neutral position, whereby should it be Γ+ or Γ-? If Γ+, you will make money if the market moves sharply one way or the other, and Γ- is the opposite: a loss no matter what. Each position has its costs: intuitively, if participants anticipate an episode of volatility, a Γ+ position will be expensive to build – you will have to actually spend money to deploy

---

[115] The graphs show a delta and a gamma of the same sign (both positive or both negative). This is not always the case just like a function and its derivative do not necessarily have the same sign.

this exposure. And if you are wrong, you will lose that investment. Classic risk/reward.

We could go much further in exploring the Greek risk management of a portfolio, notably with theta (time value) – which is expressed from one day to the next – and vega (sensitivity to volatility) – which governs the behaviour of options and the convexity of the position. But that will have to be for another day; I've set out the main principle here.

4. Why it matters

Delta management is a consequence of the Black & Scholes formula: once a closed formula is obtained to calculate the price of an option, a sensitivity analysis becomes the main risk management tool. The loop is closed: not only do non-linear payoffs deliver their secrets, but a portfolio, however complex it may be, can be managed to remain delta-neutral, i.e. relatively well protected against market movements (by choosing the risks you wish to keep and in what proportion).

The mechanics of delta, and of the Greeks more generally, allow two major advances:
- First, to analytically formalise the notion of risk. As we mentioned in the previous chapter, before Black & Scholes, the notion of convexity, while having been identified, was not easily captured in a clear mathematical frame of reference. As soon as the price of an option is derived from a closed formula, everything becomes possible. Participants can quantify randomness, simulate uncertainty and evaluate average and maximum losses; in short, reassure themselves about the *control* they can exercise over their positions. Of course, asset returns do not follow standard distribution, invalidating the Black & Scholes formula. But it is still remarkable progress compared with when you could not put even an approximate price on an option.

- Second, to efficiently and fluidly transfer risk between participants. As the market maker example illustrates, providing a price to a client is only possible if the trader can decide whether to carry the opposite risk. The more they are able to measure and hedge individual risks, the easier it is for them to provide customers with an aggressive price that corresponds exactly to what they need.

Nowadays, delta and gamma are quite simply the most fundamental levers of risk management in all trading rooms.

Conclusion

And so that brings our journey to an end, and yet the subject is so broad that this is just an introduction. Having spent much time asking myself what I should and shouldn't include, and how to present what I saw as the important concepts, a few concluding thoughts spring to mind.

First of all, I have chosen everyday examples to illustrate what seems to me an indisputable reality: we are surrounded by derivatives in our daily lives, even if they go by a different name. Arbitrage is likely to appear in various transactions (buying *primeur* wine?), and so is some form of optionality (did someone say lottery?). It is wrong to think that finance exists in an ethereal and incomprehensible universe. The financialisation of the economy is not the result of a Machiavellian plot by bankers; it is simply the consequence of our saving and consumption habits becoming more sophisticated. In other words, the supply of complexity and financial engineering has been accompanied by a widespread demand from all segments of society.

Second, it is important to put capital markets into a broader context. The banking deregulation of the 1980s and 1990s (the initial regulation being largely a result of the 1929 crisis and its devastating effects) has been well documented in the media. This deregulation has been singled out as a decisive factor in the emergence and spread of the 2008 crisis. But since 1923, and specifically the Second World War, a lot has changed. The extraordinary post-war boom led to unprecedented wealth creation. When this period ended, the consumer society borrowed beyond their means. As we discussed in Chapter 3 on interest rates, debt levels today are such that many economists wonder whether they are sustainable[116]. Savings and credit are two powerful drivers of capital markets[117]. Savings need to be invested in risk profiles that are acceptable to investors, and credit should be pooled to reduce risk. In both cases, the ultimate objective is risk control. The larger

---

[116] The accumulation of debt over the past 50 years has coincided with an uninterrupted decline in interest rates, to the point where some are now negative. What will happen when interest rates go back up?

[117] And are widely distributed among all economic agents: individuals, corporates, sovereigns. For example, corporates save through their short-term cash flows and governments through sovereign wealth funds.

the amounts, the more fluid risk circulation needs to be: no economic agent can assume a given risk single-handedly anymore, so it is crucial to divide, distribute, compartmentalise and transfer risk according to each entity's tolerance and appetite. That is what capital markets, and derivatives in particular, are for. The fundamental pillars of savings and credit are not about to disappear. Capital market finance will be no less indispensable tomorrow than it is today.

Finally, it seems appropriate to say that the hardest thing for anyone who would like to apply the principles set out in this book is to apply them *all together*. The instruments dealt with on a trading floor are not conceptually more difficult to understand than the examples we have discussed; they derive their complexity from the fact that everything must be systematically taken into consideration. Market makers who make a price for a client must worry about funding and complying with regulations in how they interact with the client, and must integrate the cost of credit lines into their price, or the initial margin of an exchange when trading a listed product. They must keep in mind the cost of capital and balance sheet restrictions, and the liquidity of the product they are trading, i.e. how difficult it might be to unwind or hedge the risk. In addition, they must operate within their risk limits at all times to ensure the integrity of their position. All this is evolving in real time, and because the market is governed by pure randomness, it is happening at varying speeds and in varying directions. Complexity is not *inherent* to market finance. After all, flying an aeroplane is hardly a cakewalk, but there's no magic involved (last time I checked!) and people learn. If this book helps to lower by even a fraction the veil of mystery that enshrouds the capital markets, it will have been a worthwhile exercise.

About the Author

An engineer from Ecole Centrale Paris and holder of an MBA from Harvard Business School, Stéphane Reverre began his career at Société Générale in Tokyo, then on the main American indices in New York. He then took responsibility for various trading activities in major financial institutions such as Lehman Brothers, Natixis, Dresdner Bank, Millennium Partners in Paris, London, Singapore and Tokyo. He is the author of a book on fundamental arbitrage techniques, "The Complete Arbitrage Deskbook", published in 2000 by McGraw-Hill.

Made in the USA
Columbia, SC
07 September 2022

66730323R00102